Investing Science

Simple, Yet Powerful.
Your Guide to Latest Strategies

Ghazwan Alemara

Copyright © 2024 Ghazwan Alemara. All rights reserved.

No part of this publication may be reproduced, distributed, or transmitted in any form or by any means, including photocopying, recording, or other electronic or mechanical methods, without the prior written permission of the publisher, except in the case of brief quotations embodied in critical reviews and certain other noncommercial uses permitted by copyright law.

For permissions requests or inquiries, please contact the publisher at hello@ghazwanalemara.com

Published by ghazwanalemara.com

Contents

Contents 3
Introduction 1
Chapter 1: The Foundations of Investing 4
    Understanding the Basics: Defining Investing 4
    The Importance of Financial Goals 6
    Types of Investments: Stocks, Bonds, and Mutual Funds 11
    Real Estate and Commodities 13
    The Risk-Return Tradeoff 19
    Diversification and its Importance 23
    The Psychology of Investing: Behavioral Finance 27
    Common Investor Biases 31
Chapter 2: Developing a Winning Strategy 37
    Setting Your Financial Goals: Short-term vs. Long-term Goals 37
    Assessing Your Risk Tolerance 40
    Crafting Your Investment Plan: Asset Allocation Strategies 44
    Creating a Diversified Portfolio 50
    The Importance of Research: Fundamental vs. Technical Analysis 54
    Evaluating Companies and Markets 58
Chapter 3: Stock Market Mastery 64
    Understanding Stocks: Types of Stocks 64
    How the Stock Market Works 69

Strategies for Stock Investment: Growth Investing 75
Value Investing 79
Advanced Stock Market Techniques: Options and Futures 83
Short Selling 87

Chapter 4: Fixed Income and Bonds 92
Basics of Bonds: What are Bonds? 92
Types of Bonds 96
Investing in Bonds: Bond Ratings and What They Mean
.... 100
Strategies for Bond Investment 105
Managing Bond Investments: Yield Curve Analysis 109
Bond Laddering 114

Chapter 5: Mutual Funds and ETFs 119
Understanding Mutual Funds: Types of Mutual Funds
.... 119
How Mutual Funds Work 124
Introduction to ETFs: What are ETFs? 129
Differences Between ETFs and Mutual Funds 133
Selecting Funds for Your Portfolio: Active vs. Passive Management 138
Evaluating Fund Performance 143

Chapter 6: Real Estate and Alternative Investments 149
Investing in Real Estate: Residential vs. Commercial Real Estate 149
REITs: Real Estate Investment Trusts 154
Commodities and Other Alternatives: Gold, Silver, and Other Commodities 159

    Cryptocurrencies and Digital Assets 164

    Benefits and Risks of Alternative Investments:
    Diversification Benefits 170

    Understanding the Risks 174

Chapter 7: Advanced Strategies and Tools 180

    Leveraging Technology in Investing: Robo-Advisors .. 180

    Using Investment Apps 185

    Quantitative Investing: Algorithmic Trading 190

    Quant Strategies 195

    Risk Management Techniques: Hedging Strategies 201

    Portfolio Insurance 206

Chapter 8: Navigating Economic and Market Cycles 211

    Understanding Economic Indicators: Key Economic
    Indicators 211

    How They Affect Investments 215

    Market Cycles and Trends: Bull and Bear Markets 221

    Identifying Market Trends 225

    Adapting to Changing Markets: Flexible Investment
    Strategies 231

    Staying Ahead of the Curve 236

Chapter 9: Building a Sustainable Investment Portfolio 242

    Principles of Sustainable Investing: ESG Criteria
    (Environmental, Social, Governance) 242

    Impact Investing 247

    Strategies for Sustainable Investing: Selecting the Right
    Investments 253

    Balancing Returns and Impact 257

    The Future of Sustainable Investing: Trends and

  Innovations 262
  Long-term Benefits 267
Chapter 10: Continuous Learning and Improvement 272
  The Importance of Financial Education: Staying Informed 273
  Continuous Learning 277
  Resources for Investors: Books, Websites, and Courses 281
  Networking and Professional Advice 286
  Reflecting on Your Investment Journey: Evaluating Your Progress 290
  Adjusting Your Strategies 294
Conclusion 300

Introduction

If you've picked up this book, you're likely eager to understand how to make your money work for you. Whether you're a beginner just dipping your toes into the world of investing or an experienced investor looking to refine your strategies, this book is designed to be your go-to guide.

Investing can often seem intimidating, with its complex jargon and fluctuating markets. However, the reality is that investing doesn't have to be overly complicated. The goal of this book is to demystify the process and provide you with clear, practical strategies that you can apply immediately. You don't need a degree in finance to understand the concepts here; all you need is the willingness to learn and the determination to achieve your financial goals.

Why "Investing Science"?

You might wonder why we chose the term "Investing Science" for this book. Science is about systematic study, observation, and experimentation. Similarly, successful investing involves research, strategy, and continuous learning. By approaching investing as a science, you can make informed decisions based on data and proven methods, rather than relying on luck or guesswork.

What You Will Learn

This book is structured to take you on a journey from the basics of investing to advanced strategies. In the beginning, we'll cover foundational topics such as understanding different types of investments and the importance of setting financial goals. As you progress, you'll learn about various investment strategies, including stocks, bonds, mutual funds, real estate, and more.

We'll also delve into modern investment tools and technologies, explore the intricacies of market cycles, and discuss how to build a sustainable investment portfolio. Each chapter is designed to be engaging and informative, breaking down complex concepts into simple, actionable insights.

A Guide for Everyone

One of the key principles of this book is accessibility. Investing should be accessible to everyone, regardless of their background or financial knowledge. Our writing style is straightforward and easy to follow, avoiding unnecessary jargon and focusing on what you need to know to succeed.

The Journey Ahead

Investing is not just about making money; it's about achieving financial freedom and security. It's about setting yourself up for a future where you can live comfortably, support your loved ones, and maybe even fulfill your dreams. This book is your companion on that journey, offering guidance, strategies, and encouragement along the way.

So, let's get started. Turn the page, and take the first step toward mastering the science of investing. Your financial future awaits.

Chapter 1: The Foundations of Investing

Understanding the Basics: Defining Investing

Investing is the act of allocating money or resources with the expectation of generating an income or profit. At its core, investing is about making your money work for you, rather than just letting it sit in a bank account. This can be done through various means such as purchasing stocks, bonds, real estate, or other financial instruments.

When you invest, you are essentially buying a piece of a company, a share in a bond, or a portion of a property. The goal is to benefit from the growth and earnings of these assets over time. For example, if you buy shares in a company and the company performs well, the value of your shares increases. Similarly, if you invest in a bond, you earn interest on the money you lent to the bond issuer.

Investing differs from saving in that it typically involves a higher level of risk but also offers the potential for higher returns. Savings accounts, while safe, usually offer lower returns compared to investments. This is because savings are generally kept in secure, low-risk accounts, whereas investments are subject to market fluctuations and economic changes.

One key aspect of investing is understanding the concept of risk and return. Every investment carries some level of risk—the possibility that you may lose some or all of the money you invest. However, higher risk often comes with the potential for higher returns. For instance, stocks are generally riskier than bonds, but they also tend to offer greater returns over the long term.

Another important concept in investing is diversification. This means spreading your investments across different types of assets to reduce risk. By diversifying, you are not putting all your eggs in one basket. If one investment performs poorly, others may perform well, balancing out your overall returns.

Investing also involves a time horizon, which is the period you expect to hold an investment before needing to access your money. Different investments are suited to different time horizons. Stocks, for example, are better for long-term goals, while bonds may be more appropriate for medium-term goals.

The psychology of investing plays a significant role in how successful you are as an investor. Emotions like fear and greed can influence investment decisions, often leading to poor outcomes. It's important to stay disciplined, do your research, and avoid making impulsive decisions based on market fluctuations.

Overall, investing is a powerful tool for building wealth and achieving financial goals. By understanding the basics and developing a well-thought-out strategy, you can make informed decisions that help you grow your money over time.

The Importance of Financial Goals

Setting financial goals is a crucial first step in your investment journey. Without clear goals, it's easy to lose direction and make impulsive decisions that may not serve your long-term interests. Think of financial goals as a roadmap guiding you toward your desired future. They help you stay focused, motivated, and on track to achieve financial success.

Why Set Financial Goals?

Financial goals give you a sense of purpose and direction. When you know what you're aiming for, it's easier to make informed decisions and take the necessary actions to reach your objectives. Goals help you prioritize your spending, saving, and investing, ensuring that your financial resources are used effectively.

For example, if you have a goal of buying a home in five years, you can tailor your investment strategy to accumulate the necessary down payment. Without this goal, you might spend money on things that don't contribute to your long-term financial well-being.

Types of Financial Goals

Financial goals can be categorized into short-term, medium-term, and long-term goals. Short-term goals are those you aim to achieve within a year, such as building an emergency fund or paying off high-interest debt. Medium-term goals, which typically span one to five years, might include saving for a vacation or purchasing a car. Long-term goals often extend beyond five years and include major life events like retirement or funding your children's education.

Each type of goal requires a different approach and investment strategy. Short-term goals might be best served by low-risk, easily accessible investments, while long-term goals can afford to take on more risk for potentially higher returns.

Setting SMART Goals

A helpful framework for setting financial goals is the SMART criteria. SMART stands for Specific, Measurable, Achievable, Relevant, and Time-bound. Let's break down each component:

- **Specific**: Clearly define your goal. Instead of saying, "I want to save money," specify, "I want to save $10,000 for a down payment on a house."

- **Measurable**: Make sure your goal is quantifiable. This allows you to track your progress and stay motivated.

- **Achievable**: Set realistic goals that you can attain with effort and discipline. An unachievable goal can be discouraging.

- **Relevant**: Ensure your goals align with your broader financial aspirations and life values.

- **Time-bound**: Set a deadline for achieving your goal. A timeline creates a sense of urgency and helps you stay focused.

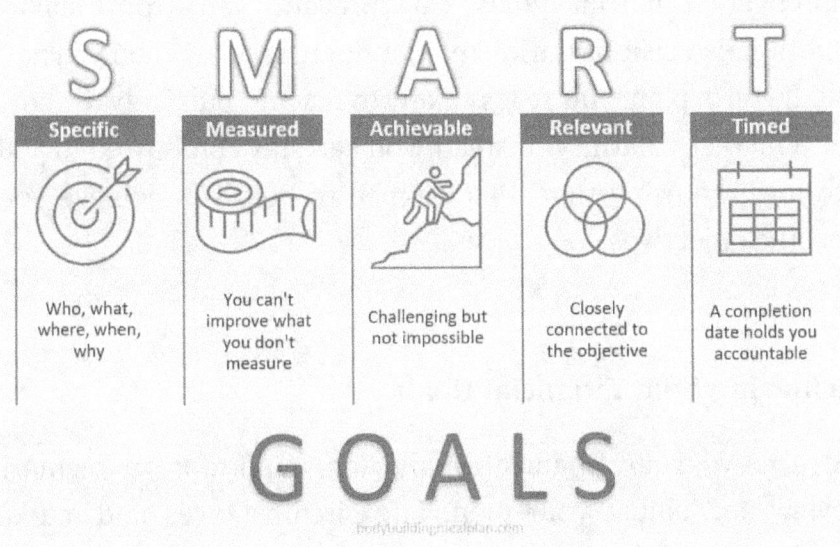

SMART Goals Framework. Source: wnccumc.org

The Role of Financial Goals in Investing

Investing without clear goals is like setting out on a journey without a destination. Financial goals inform your investment decisions and strategy. They help you determine the appropriate asset allocation, risk tolerance, and investment horizon. For instance, if your goal is to retire in 30 years, you might choose a diversified portfolio with a mix of stocks and bonds that balances growth and stability.

Moreover, financial goals can prevent you from making emotional decisions during market fluctuations. When you have a long-term plan, you're less likely to react impulsively to short-term market volatility. Instead, you can stay committed to your strategy, knowing that it's designed to help you achieve your specific objectives.

Achieving Your Financial Goals

To achieve your financial goals, it's important to regularly review and adjust your plan. Life circumstances and market conditions can change, and your goals might need to be updated accordingly. Regularly monitoring your progress ensures that you stay on track and make necessary adjustments to stay aligned with your objectives.

In conclusion, setting financial goals is essential for successful investing. Clear, well-defined goals provide direction, motivation, and a framework for making informed investment decisions. They help you prioritize your financial activities and stay focused on what truly matters. By setting and working toward your financial goals, you pave the way for a secure and prosperous future.

Types of Investments: Stocks, Bonds, and Mutual Funds

When it comes to investing, three of the most common options you'll hear about are stocks, bonds, and mutual funds. Each of these investment types has its own characteristics, risks, and potential returns, making them suitable for different kinds of investors and financial goals.

Stocks

Stocks represent ownership in a company. When you buy a stock, you purchase a small piece of that company, known as a share. As a shareholder, you can benefit in two main ways: through price appreciation and dividends. Price appreciation occurs when the value of the stock increases over time, allowing you to sell it for a profit. Dividends are regular payments made to shareholders from the company's earnings.

Investing in stocks can be rewarding, but it comes with a higher level of risk. Stock prices can fluctuate significantly based on a variety of factors, including the company's performance, industry trends, and overall market conditions. This volatility means that while you have the potential for high returns, you also face the possibility of losing money.

Bonds

Bonds are essentially loans you make to a government or corporation in exchange for periodic interest payments and the return of the bond's face value when it matures. Bonds are generally considered safer than stocks because they provide a fixed income and are less volatile. However, the returns on bonds are usually lower than those on stocks.

There are different types of bonds, including government bonds, corporate bonds, and municipal bonds. Government bonds, such as U.S. Treasury bonds, are considered very safe but offer lower returns. Corporate bonds tend to offer higher returns but come with more risk, especially if the issuing company has financial troubles. Municipal bonds are issued by state or local governments and often come with tax benefits.

Mutual Funds

Mutual funds pool money from many investors to purchase a diversified portfolio of stocks, bonds, or other securities. When you invest in a mutual fund, you buy shares of the fund, and your money is managed by professional fund managers. This makes mutual funds an attractive option for investors who prefer a hands-off approach.

One of the main advantages of mutual funds is diversification. Because mutual funds invest in a variety of assets, they spread risk across multiple investments. This reduces the impact of any single investment performing poorly. Mutual funds also come in many varieties, such as equity funds, which invest primarily in stocks, and bond funds, which focus on bonds.

However, mutual funds come with fees, such as management fees and expense ratios, which can eat into your returns. It's important to understand these costs and how they affect your investment.

Each of these investment types—stocks, bonds, and mutual funds—has its own set of advantages and disadvantages. Your choice will depend on your financial goals, risk tolerance, and investment horizon. By understanding how each works, you can make more informed decisions and build a well-rounded investment portfolio.

Real Estate and Commodities

Investing in real estate and commodities can be an excellent way to diversify your investment portfolio. These asset classes offer unique opportunities and benefits that can help balance the risks and rewards associated with traditional investments like stocks and bonds. Let's explore how you can incorporate real estate and commodities into your investment strategy.

Investing in Real Estate

Real estate investment involves purchasing property to generate income or appreciation. It can be a lucrative investment, providing both regular income through rental payments and potential appreciation in property value over time. Here are some key aspects of real estate investing:

Residential Real Estate: This includes single-family homes, apartments, and condos. Investors typically buy these properties to rent them out and earn a steady income. The demand for rental properties can be strong, especially in urban areas with high population density.

Commercial Real Estate: This encompasses office buildings, retail spaces, warehouses, and industrial properties. Commercial properties often have longer lease agreements than residential properties, providing a more stable income stream. However, they may also require a higher initial investment and can be affected by economic cycles.

Real Estate Investment Trusts (REITs): REITs allow you to invest in real estate without having to buy property directly. These companies own, operate, or finance income-generating real estate and pay dividends to shareholders. REITs can be a good option for investors looking for liquidity and diversification without the hassle of property management.

Benefits of Real Estate Investing

Real estate can provide several advantages, including:

- **Income Generation**: Rental properties can offer a consistent income stream, which can be particularly attractive during times of stock market volatility.

- **Appreciation Potential**: Real estate values can increase over time, providing capital gains when you sell the property.

- **Inflation Hedge**: Real estate often keeps pace with inflation, as property values and rents tend to rise with the cost of living.

- **Diversification**: Adding real estate to your portfolio can help spread risk across different asset classes.

Risks of Real Estate Investing

While real estate can be profitable, it also comes with risks:

- **Liquidity**: Real estate is not as easily bought or sold as stocks or bonds, which can make it difficult to quickly access your invested capital.

- **Market Risk**: Property values can decline due to economic downturns, changes in the local market, or other factors.

- **Management and Maintenance**: Owning property requires ongoing management and upkeep, which can be time-consuming and costly.

Investing in Commodities

Commodities are raw materials or primary agricultural products that can be bought and sold, such as gold, oil, or wheat. Investing in commodities can be a way to protect against inflation and diversify your investment portfolio. Here are some common types of commodities investments:

Precious Metals: Gold, silver, platinum, and palladium are popular investments due to their intrinsic value and use as a store of wealth. These metals can provide a hedge against inflation and economic uncertainty.

Energy Commodities: Oil, natural gas, and coal are essential resources for the global economy. Investing in energy commodities can offer exposure to the energy sector and potential growth as demand for energy increases.

Agricultural Commodities: Corn, wheat, soybeans, and livestock are examples of agricultural commodities. These investments can benefit from global population growth and changing dietary trends.

Benefits of Commodities Investing

Commodities can enhance your portfolio by offering:

- **Inflation Protection**: Commodity prices often rise with inflation, helping to preserve purchasing power.

- **Diversification**: Commodities tend to have a low correlation with traditional asset classes, providing diversification benefits.

- **Tangible Assets**: Commodities are physical assets with intrinsic value, offering a sense of security for investors.

Risks of Commodities Investing

Investing in commodities also involves risks:

- **Volatility**: Commodity prices can be highly volatile due to factors like supply and demand, geopolitical events, and weather conditions.

- **Storage and Transportation**: Physical commodities require storage and transportation, which can add costs and logistical challenges.

- **Market Risk**: Commodities markets can be influenced by economic cycles, policy changes, and technological advancements.

Balancing Real Estate and Commodities in Your Portfolio

To effectively incorporate real estate and commodities into your portfolio, consider your financial goals, risk tolerance, and investment horizon. These asset classes can provide diversification and potential returns, but they also come with unique challenges and risks. By carefully selecting and managing your investments, you can enhance your portfolio's overall performance and achieve greater financial stability.

Real estate and commodities offer valuable opportunities for investors willing to explore beyond traditional investments. With careful planning and a clear understanding of the market, you can make these asset classes work for you, helping you build a robust and diversified investment portfolio.

The Risk-Return Tradeoff

The risk-return tradeoff is a fundamental concept in investing that you need to understand to make informed decisions. Simply put, it's the relationship between the potential risk you take on an investment and the potential return you can expect to earn from it.

At the heart of this tradeoff is the principle that higher returns come with higher risks. If an investment offers the possibility of substantial gains, it typically also comes with a greater chance of losing money. Conversely, investments that are considered safe generally offer lower returns.

Understanding Risk

Risk in investing refers to the uncertainty about the outcome of an investment. This uncertainty means that the actual return on an investment can differ from the expected return. There are several types of risk to be aware of:

- **Market Risk:** The risk of losses due to factors that affect the overall performance of the financial markets.

- **Credit Risk:** The risk that a bond issuer will default and be unable to make interest payments or repay the principal.

- **Inflation Risk:** The risk that the return on an investment will not keep up with inflation, eroding purchasing power.

- **Interest Rate Risk:** The risk that changes in interest rates will negatively affect the value of bonds or other fixed-income investments.

Understanding these risks helps you gauge how much uncertainty you can handle and how it might impact your financial goals.

Understanding Return

Return is the profit or loss you earn from an investment over a certain period. It can come in various forms, such as capital gains (an increase in the value of an asset), dividends (payments from stocks), or interest (payments from bonds). When evaluating an investment, you'll often look at the expected return, which is an estimate of the potential profit based on historical performance or other factors.

Balancing Risk and Return

The key to successful investing is finding the right balance between risk and return that aligns with your financial goals and risk tolerance. Here are a few strategies to consider:

- **Diversification:** Spread your investments across different asset classes (stocks, bonds, real estate, etc.) to reduce risk. If one investment performs poorly, others may perform well, balancing your overall return.

- **Asset Allocation:** Allocate your investments based on your risk tolerance and time horizon. For example, younger investors with a longer time horizon might invest more heavily in stocks, while those closer to retirement might focus more on bonds and other safer investments.

- **Regular Review:** Continuously monitor and adjust your portfolio as needed to ensure it remains aligned with your goals and risk tolerance. Market conditions and your personal circumstances can change, so your investment strategy might need to evolve over time.

Personal Risk Tolerance

Everyone has a different level of risk tolerance based on factors like age, income, financial goals, and personality. Assessing your risk tolerance honestly is crucial. If you're uncomfortable with the idea of losing money in the short term, you might prefer more conservative investments. On the other hand, if you can tolerate short-term losses for the potential of higher long-term gains, you might lean towards more aggressive investments.

Understanding the risk-return tradeoff helps you make more informed investment decisions. By recognizing how much risk you're willing to take and what kind of returns you expect, you can build a portfolio that aims to achieve your financial goals while staying within your comfort zone.

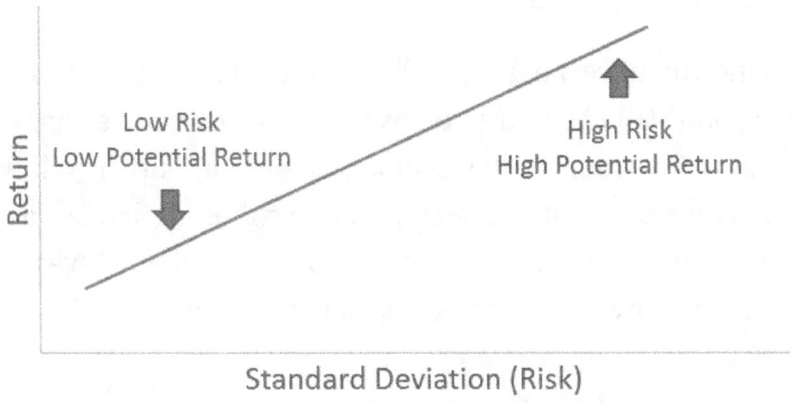

The Risk-Return Tradeoff. Source: modelinvesting.com

Diversification and its Importance

Diversification is a fundamental principle of investing that involves spreading your investments across various asset classes, industries, and geographic regions. The primary goal of diversification is to reduce risk by ensuring that your portfolio is not overly reliant on the performance of a single investment or market segment. By diversifying, you can protect your investments from significant losses and increase the potential for steady returns over time.

Understanding Diversification

Imagine you have a basket of different fruits. If one type of fruit spoils, you still have other types to enjoy. Diversification works similarly for your investments. Instead of putting all your money into one stock or asset, you distribute it across various investments. This way, the poor performance of one investment can be offset by the better performance of others.

Benefits of Diversification

One of the main benefits of diversification is risk reduction. When your investments are spread out, the impact of a single asset's poor performance on your overall portfolio is minimized. This is particularly important in volatile markets, where individual asset prices can fluctuate significantly.

Diversification also offers the potential for more stable returns. Since different asset classes often perform differently under various market conditions, having a mix of investments can help balance your portfolio. For example, when stocks are performing poorly, bonds might do well, thereby cushioning the overall impact on your portfolio.

Additionally, diversification allows you to take advantage of growth opportunities across different sectors and regions. By investing in a variety of assets, you increase your chances of benefiting from market upswings in different areas.

How to Diversify Your Portfolio

Diversifying your portfolio doesn't have to be complicated. Here are some straightforward strategies:

Spread Your Investments Across Asset Classes: Include a mix of stocks, bonds, real estate, and commodities in your portfolio. Each asset class responds differently to economic changes, helping to stabilize your overall returns.

Invest in Different Sectors: Don't put all your money into one industry. Instead, spread your investments across various sectors such as technology, healthcare, finance, and consumer goods. This helps protect your portfolio from industry-specific downturns.

Consider Geographic Diversification: Invest in both domestic and international markets. Economic conditions can vary significantly from one country to another, so having a global portfolio can provide additional protection and opportunities.

Use Mutual Funds and ETFs: These investment vehicles allow you to easily diversify by pooling money from many investors to buy a broad range of assets. They are an excellent way to gain exposure to different markets and sectors without needing to buy individual securities.

Balancing Risk and Reward

While diversification helps reduce risk, it's important to balance it with your investment goals and risk tolerance. Over-diversifying can dilute your returns, making it harder to achieve your financial objectives. It's crucial to find the right balance, ensuring you have enough diversification to protect your portfolio but not so much that it hampers your growth potential.

Regularly reviewing and rebalancing your portfolio is key to maintaining effective diversification. As market conditions change, the value of your investments will fluctuate, potentially altering your asset allocation. By periodically adjusting your portfolio, you can ensure it remains aligned with your goals and risk tolerance.

The Role of Diversification in Long-Term Success

Diversification is not just about protecting your portfolio from short-term losses. It's a long-term strategy that helps build wealth gradually and sustainably. By spreading your investments, you reduce the impact of market volatility and create a more resilient portfolio capable of weathering economic downturns.

Ultimately, diversification is about making smart investment choices that align with your financial goals and risk tolerance. It's a strategy that helps you manage risk, capitalize on growth opportunities, and achieve more stable returns over time. Whether you're a novice investor or an experienced one, diversification should be a cornerstone of your investment approach, guiding you toward a more secure and prosperous financial future.

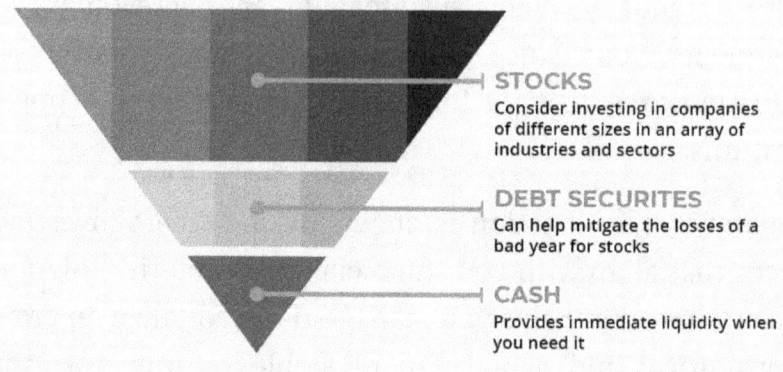

Simple Diversification. Source: pacificlife.com

The Psychology of Investing: Behavioral Finance

Behavioral finance is a field that combines psychology and economics to explain why and how people make irrational financial decisions. Traditional finance theories assume that investors are rational and always make decisions that maximize their wealth. However, behavioral finance recognizes that investors are often influenced by emotions and cognitive biases, leading them to make suboptimal choices.

Common Behavioral Biases

Several biases can affect investment decisions. Understanding these can help you recognize when your own thinking might be leading you astray.

Overconfidence Bias

Overconfidence is when investors overestimate their knowledge, abilities, and the accuracy of their information. This can lead to excessive trading, underestimating risks, and eventually, lower returns. For instance, an overconfident investor might believe they can consistently pick winning stocks, leading to a lack of diversification and increased vulnerability to market volatility.

Anchoring Bias

Anchoring occurs when investors rely too heavily on the first piece of information they encounter (the "anchor") when making decisions. For example, if an investor buys a stock at $50 and it drops to $40, they might hold onto it, waiting for it to return to the purchase price, rather than reassessing its current value and future potential.

Herding Behavior

Herding is the tendency to follow the actions of a larger group, often leading to market bubbles and crashes. Investors might buy into a rapidly rising stock simply because others are doing so, without conducting their own research. This can inflate prices beyond the stock's actual value, eventually leading to a sharp decline.

Loss Aversion

Loss aversion is the tendency to prefer avoiding losses rather than acquiring equivalent gains. It's rooted in the idea that the pain of losing is psychologically twice as powerful as the pleasure of gaining. This can lead to holding onto losing investments too long, hoping they will rebound, rather than cutting losses and reallocating resources to more promising opportunities.

Confirmation Bias

Confirmation bias is the tendency to search for, interpret, and remember information that confirms one's preconceptions, while ignoring evidence that contradicts them. An investor might focus on positive news about a favored stock while disregarding negative reports, leading to an imbalanced view and potentially poor investment decisions.

Mitigating Behavioral Biases

Recognizing and mitigating these biases can improve your investment outcomes. Here are some strategies to help:

- **Stay Informed and Educated:** Continuously educate yourself about financial markets and investment strategies. The more knowledgeable you are, the less likely you are to rely on gut feelings and biases.

- **Develop a Plan and Stick to It:** Create a well-thought-out investment plan based on your financial goals, risk tolerance, and time horizon. Having a plan helps you stay disciplined and resist the urge to make impulsive decisions.

- **Diversify Your Investments:** Diversification reduces the impact of any single investment performing poorly and helps mitigate the risk of emotional decision-making.

- **Regularly Review and Rebalance Your Portfolio:** Periodically review your investment portfolio to ensure it remains aligned with your goals and risk tolerance. Rebalancing helps you maintain your desired asset allocation and reduces the influence of short-term market fluctuations.

- **Seek Professional Advice:** Consider working with a financial advisor who can provide objective guidance and help you make informed decisions. An advisor can offer a fresh perspective and counterbalance your emotional impulses.

By understanding behavioral finance, you can become more aware of the psychological factors that influence your investment decisions. This awareness can help you make more rational, objective choices, ultimately leading to better financial outcomes.

Common Investor Biases

Investing is as much about managing your emotions and psychology as it is about understanding markets and analyzing data. Human nature can often lead to biases that impact investment decisions, sometimes to the detriment of our financial goals. Recognizing and understanding these common biases can help you make more rational and effective investment choices.

Overconfidence Bias

Overconfidence bias is when investors overestimate their knowledge, abilities, or control over outcomes. This can lead to excessive trading, taking on too much risk, or ignoring valuable advice and information. Overconfident investors might believe they can predict market movements accurately or that their investment choices are infallible, which can result in significant losses.

Confirmation Bias

Confirmation bias occurs when investors seek out information that confirms their existing beliefs while ignoring or undervaluing information that contradicts them. This can create a skewed perspective and reinforce poor investment choices. For example, an investor who believes a particular stock will perform well might only pay attention to positive news about the company and dismiss any negative reports, leading to an imbalanced view.

Herd Mentality

Herd mentality is the tendency to follow the actions of a larger group, often driven by the fear of missing out or the belief that the majority is always right. This can lead to buying assets at inflated prices during market bubbles or selling in panic during downturns. Following the crowd can sometimes result in suboptimal investment decisions, as the broader market sentiment doesn't always reflect fundamental values.

Loss Aversion

Loss aversion is the tendency to prefer avoiding losses over acquiring equivalent gains. This bias can lead to overly conservative investment strategies or the reluctance to sell losing investments in the hope they will rebound. The fear of realizing a loss can prevent investors from making necessary adjustments to their portfolios, potentially locking in further declines.

Anchoring Bias

Anchoring bias occurs when investors rely too heavily on the first piece of information they receive (the "anchor") when making decisions. For example, if an investor buys a stock at a certain price, they might fixate on that price as the stock's true value, even if new information suggests otherwise. This can hinder their ability to make objective decisions based on current data.

Recency Bias

Recency bias is the tendency to give undue weight to recent events or trends when making investment decisions. Investors might assume that a recent market rally will continue indefinitely or that a recent decline signals a long-term downturn. This bias can lead to short-term thinking and reactions that may not align with a well-thought-out investment strategy.

Familiarity Bias

Familiarity bias leads investors to favor investments they are familiar with, such as local companies or industries they work in. While this can sometimes provide an informational advantage, it can also result in a lack of diversification and an over-concentration in specific sectors. Diversifying across unfamiliar assets and markets can often provide better risk-adjusted returns.

Strategies to Mitigate Biases

Awareness is the first step in mitigating the impact of these biases. Here are a few strategies to help you make more objective investment decisions:

- **Educate Yourself**: Continuously learning about markets, investment strategies, and financial principles can help counteract biases.

- **Set Clear Goals and Plans**: Having a well-defined investment plan aligned with your long-term goals can provide a framework to guide your decisions, reducing the influence of emotions.

- **Diversify**: Spread your investments across various asset classes, sectors, and geographic regions to reduce the risk associated with specific biases.

- **Seek Advice**: Consulting with financial advisors or trusted peers can provide different perspectives and help counterbalance your biases.

- **Reflect and Review**: Regularly reviewing your investment decisions and outcomes can help you recognize patterns of bias and adjust your approach accordingly.

By being mindful of these common investor biases and implementing strategies to mitigate their effects, you can improve your decision-making process and enhance your chances of achieving your financial objectives.

Chapter 2: Developing a Winning Strategy

Setting Your Financial Goals: Short-term vs. Long-term Goals

When it comes to investing, setting clear financial goals is crucial. Understanding the difference between short-term and long-term goals can help you make better investment decisions and choose the right strategies for achieving them.

Short-term Goals

Short-term goals are financial objectives you aim to achieve within the next few months to a few years. Examples include saving for a vacation, building an emergency fund, or making a down payment on a car. Because the timeframe for these goals is relatively short, the primary focus should be on preserving capital and ensuring liquidity.

Investments for short-term goals should be low-risk and easily accessible. High-yield savings accounts, money market funds, and short-term bonds are common choices. These options provide stability and allow you to access your money when needed without worrying about significant market fluctuations.

For instance, if you're saving for a wedding in a year, you wouldn't want to invest in volatile stocks that might drop in value right when you need the money. Instead, a savings account or a short-term certificate of deposit (CD) would be more appropriate, offering safety and modest interest.

Long-term Goals

Long-term goals, on the other hand, are objectives set for a more extended period, typically five years or more. Examples include retirement savings, funding your child's college education, or buying a home. Since you have more time to achieve these goals, you can afford to take on more risk, potentially earning higher returns.

Investments for long-term goals often include stocks, real estate, and mutual funds. These assets may be more volatile in the short term, but they tend to offer higher growth potential over the long haul. The idea is that the longer time horizon allows you to ride out market ups and downs, increasing the likelihood of achieving substantial growth.

For example, if you're planning for retirement 30 years from now, investing in a diversified portfolio of stocks and bonds can help you build wealth over time. The stock market might have bad years, but historically, it has trended upward over decades.

Balancing Short-term and Long-term Goals

It's important to balance your short-term and long-term goals, ensuring you're adequately preparing for both. This might mean allocating a portion of your income to a savings account for short-term needs while contributing regularly to a retirement account for long-term security.

One strategy to manage this balance is to create a financial plan that outlines your goals and the steps needed to achieve them. This plan should include a budget that allocates funds towards both types of goals. Regularly reviewing and adjusting your plan can help you stay on track and make informed decisions as your financial situation evolves.

By clearly distinguishing between short-term and long-term goals, you can choose appropriate investment vehicles and strategies that align with your objectives and timeframes. This approach ensures that you're not only prepared for immediate needs but also building a solid foundation for your future.

Assessing Your Risk Tolerance

Understanding your risk tolerance is a vital part of developing a successful investment strategy. Risk tolerance refers to the degree of variability in investment returns that you are willing to withstand. It's a personal measure that varies from one investor to another, influenced by various factors such as financial goals, time horizon, and emotional comfort with market fluctuations.

What is Risk Tolerance?

Risk tolerance is essentially how much risk you can handle without losing sleep. It encompasses both your ability to take on risk (based on financial capacity) and your willingness to take on risk (based on your psychological comfort). Some investors are comfortable with the ups and downs of the stock market, while others prefer the stability of more conservative investments.

Factors Influencing Risk Tolerance

Several factors can influence your risk tolerance, including:

Financial Goals: Your investment objectives play a significant role in determining your risk tolerance. If you are investing for long-term goals like retirement, you may be able to accept more risk for the potential of higher returns. Conversely, if you are saving for a short-term goal, like buying a house in the next few years, you might prefer lower-risk investments to preserve your capital.

Time Horizon: The amount of time you plan to invest before needing the money affects your risk tolerance. A longer time horizon allows you to ride out market volatility and recover from downturns, making it easier to take on more risk. A shorter time horizon requires more conservative investments to ensure the money is available when you need it.

Financial Situation: Your current financial health, including your income, expenses, savings, and debt levels, influences your ability to take on risk. If you have a stable income and substantial savings, you might be more comfortable with higher-risk investments. If your financial situation is more precarious, lower-risk options might be more appropriate.

Personal Comfort: Emotional factors and personality traits also play a crucial role. Some people are naturally more risk-averse and feel anxious about market fluctuations, while others may enjoy the thrill of taking risks and are more comfortable with the potential for higher volatility.

How to Assess Your Risk Tolerance

To assess your risk tolerance, consider the following steps:

Reflect on Past Experiences: Think about how you have reacted to financial decisions and market changes in the past. Did you stay calm during market downturns, or did you feel anxious and want to sell your investments? Your past behavior can provide valuable insights into your risk tolerance.

Evaluate Your Financial Goals: Clearly define your short-term and long-term financial goals. Understanding what you are investing for can help you determine how much risk you need to take to achieve those goals.

Analyze Your Time Horizon: Assess how long you plan to keep your investments. A longer investment horizon generally allows for a higher risk tolerance, as you have more time to recover from potential losses.

Consider Your Financial Stability: Review your current financial situation, including your income, savings, and debt. Ensure that you have an emergency fund and that your essential expenses are covered before taking on higher-risk investments.

Use Risk Tolerance Questionnaires: Many financial institutions and advisors offer risk tolerance questionnaires that can help you evaluate your comfort level with different types of investments. These tools ask questions about your investment goals, time horizon, and reactions to market scenarios to provide a more objective assessment.

Matching Investments to Your Risk Tolerance

Once you have a clear understanding of your risk tolerance, you can select investments that align with your comfort level. For example:

Conservative Investor: If you have a low risk tolerance, you might prefer investments like bonds, dividend-paying stocks, and money market funds that offer stability and lower volatility.

Moderate Investor: If you are comfortable with a moderate level of risk, a balanced portfolio with a mix of stocks and bonds might be suitable. This approach offers potential growth while managing risk.

Aggressive Investor: If you have a high risk tolerance, you might be willing to invest in high-growth stocks, international markets, and other volatile assets that offer the potential for significant returns.

Assessing your risk tolerance is a dynamic process. It's important to review it periodically, especially as your financial goals, time horizon, and personal circumstances change. By understanding and respecting your risk tolerance, you can make informed investment decisions that help you achieve your financial goals while maintaining your peace of mind.

Crafting Your Investment Plan: Asset Allocation Strategies

Asset allocation is the process of spreading your investments across different asset classes, such as stocks, bonds, and cash, to manage risk and achieve your financial goals. The right asset allocation strategy balances risk and reward based on your individual circumstances, such as your risk tolerance, time horizon, and financial objectives.

Understanding Asset Classes

Different asset classes behave differently under various market conditions. Stocks, for instance, are generally more volatile but offer higher potential returns. Bonds tend to be more stable and provide regular income but with lower growth potential. Cash and cash equivalents, like money market funds, offer the least risk but also the least return.

The Importance of Diversification

Diversification involves spreading your investments across various asset classes and within each class to reduce risk. The idea is that different assets will respond differently to the same economic event. For example, when stock prices fall, bond prices might rise, balancing out your portfolio's overall performance.

Strategic Asset Allocation

Strategic asset allocation is a long-term approach where you set target allocations for each asset class and periodically rebalance your portfolio to maintain these targets. This strategy is based on your risk tolerance and investment goals.

For instance, a young investor with a high risk tolerance and a long time horizon might allocate 80% to stocks and 20% to bonds. Over time, as stocks outperform bonds, this allocation might shift to 85% stocks and 15% bonds. Rebalancing would involve selling some stocks and buying bonds to return to the original 80/20 mix.

Tactical Asset Allocation

Tactical asset allocation allows for a more flexible approach. Investors might shift their asset allocation based on short-term market conditions or economic forecasts. This strategy requires more active management and a willingness to take on higher risk in pursuit of higher returns.

For example, if economic indicators suggest a strong upcoming performance for the technology sector, you might temporarily increase your allocation to tech stocks. Once the sector's performance normalizes, you would readjust your portfolio to your original asset mix.

Dynamic Asset Allocation

Dynamic asset allocation is a more aggressive strategy that frequently adjusts the mix of assets as markets rise and fall. This approach requires constant monitoring and a deep understanding of market trends. It's best suited for experienced investors who can handle frequent trading and the associated risks.

Life-Cycle or Target-Date Funds

These funds automatically adjust their asset allocation based on a specific target date, such as retirement. Early on, the fund might be heavily weighted towards stocks. As the target date approaches, it gradually shifts towards more conservative investments like bonds and cash. This strategy simplifies the asset allocation process for investors who prefer a hands-off approach.

Personalizing Your Asset Allocation

Your asset allocation should reflect your individual risk tolerance, financial goals, and investment horizon. A conservative investor focused on preserving capital might prefer a mix with more bonds and cash, while an aggressive investor seeking growth might lean heavily towards stocks.

For instance, if you're saving for a down payment on a house in five years, you might want a conservative allocation, emphasizing stability and low risk. Conversely, if you're investing for retirement 30 years away, you can afford to take on more risk with a higher stock allocation.

Regularly Review and Rebalance

It's essential to review your asset allocation regularly to ensure it remains aligned with your goals. Life events, changes in your financial situation, or significant market movements might necessitate adjustments. Rebalancing your portfolio involves selling some assets and buying others to maintain your desired allocation, keeping your investment plan on track.

By understanding and implementing effective asset allocation strategies, you can manage risk and optimize returns, paving the way to achieving your financial goals.

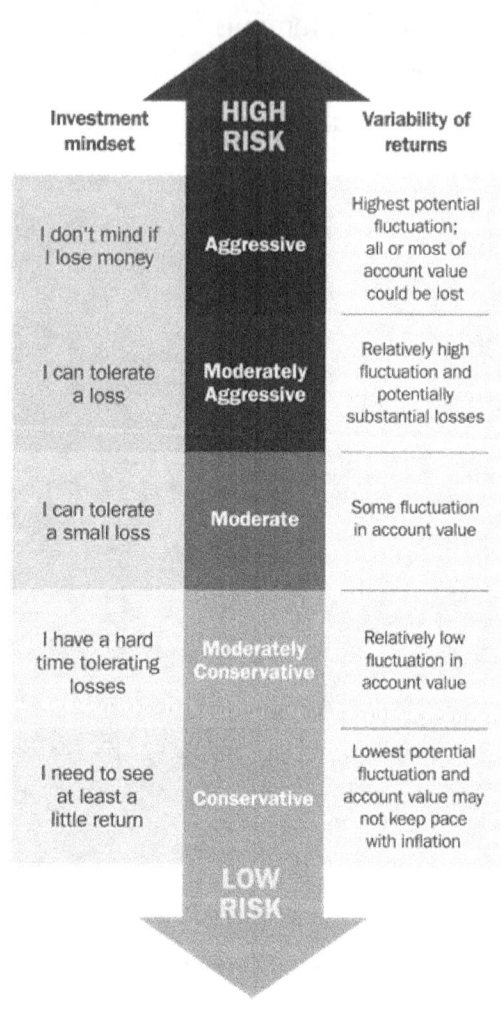

Risk Tolerance Spectrum. Source: ameripriseadvisors.com

Creating a Diversified Portfolio

Creating a diversified portfolio is essential for managing risk and achieving your long-term financial goals. Diversification involves spreading your investments across different asset classes, industries, and geographical regions to reduce the impact of any single investment's poor performance on your overall portfolio. A well-diversified portfolio can provide more stable returns and help you navigate various market conditions.

Understanding Asset Classes

To build a diversified portfolio, it's important to understand the different asset classes available to you. The main asset classes include:

Stocks: Investing in stocks means buying shares of publicly traded companies. Stocks offer the potential for high returns but come with higher risk due to market volatility.

Bonds: Bonds are essentially loans you give to governments or corporations in exchange for periodic interest payments and the return of the principal amount at maturity. Bonds are generally considered lower risk than stocks and provide more stable income.

Real Estate: Real estate investments include residential and commercial properties. These investments can generate rental income and appreciate over time. Real estate can act as a hedge against inflation.

Commodities: Commodities are physical goods like gold, oil, and agricultural products. They can provide diversification and protection against inflation but tend to be more volatile.

Cash and Cash Equivalents: This category includes savings accounts, money market funds, and certificates of deposit (CDs). These are the safest investments, offering stability and liquidity but lower returns.

Diversifying Within Asset Classes

Diversification doesn't stop at spreading investments across different asset classes. It's also important to diversify within each class. For example, within your stock investments, you can diversify by investing in companies across various industries such as technology, healthcare, finance, and consumer goods. This helps mitigate the risk of a downturn in any single industry.

Similarly, within bonds, you can invest in government bonds, corporate bonds, and municipal bonds with varying maturities and credit ratings. This approach balances the risk and return characteristics of your bond investments.

Geographical Diversification

Geographical diversification involves investing in assets from different countries and regions. This helps reduce the risk associated with economic or political issues in any single country. By including international stocks and bonds in your portfolio, you can benefit from growth opportunities in emerging markets and developed economies alike.

Investment Vehicles for Diversification

There are various investment vehicles that can help you achieve diversification efficiently:

Mutual Funds: Mutual funds pool money from many investors to buy a diversified portfolio of stocks, bonds, or other securities. They offer instant diversification and are managed by professional fund managers.

Exchange-Traded Funds (ETFs): ETFs are similar to mutual funds but trade on stock exchanges like individual stocks. They provide diversification and flexibility, allowing you to buy and sell shares throughout the trading day.

Index Funds: Index funds aim to replicate the performance of a specific market index, such as the S&P 500. They offer broad market exposure and low fees, making them a popular choice for diversification.

Balancing Your Portfolio

Once you have selected your investments, it's crucial to maintain the right balance. Your asset allocation should align with your risk tolerance, financial goals, and time horizon. For instance, a younger investor with a higher risk tolerance and a long-term investment horizon might allocate more towards stocks, while an older investor nearing retirement might prefer a higher allocation to bonds and cash equivalents.

Regularly reviewing and rebalancing your portfolio ensures that it remains aligned with your investment strategy. Market fluctuations can cause your asset allocation to drift from your target mix. Rebalancing involves selling overperforming assets and buying underperforming ones to restore your desired allocation.

Benefits of a Diversified Portfolio

A diversified portfolio can help you achieve more consistent returns and reduce the risk of significant losses. By spreading your investments across various assets, industries, and regions, you are less likely to be severely affected by poor performance in any single area. Diversification also allows you to capture growth opportunities across different markets, enhancing your overall return potential.

Creating a diversified portfolio is a fundamental aspect of sound investment practice. It helps manage risk, stabilize returns, and achieve your long-term financial goals. By understanding and applying the principles of diversification, you can build a robust investment strategy that stands the test of time.

The Importance of Research: Fundamental vs. Technical Analysis

Investing in the stock market involves making informed decisions about which stocks to buy, hold, or sell. Two primary methods for evaluating stocks are fundamental analysis and technical analysis. Understanding these approaches can help you develop a more effective investment strategy.

Fundamental Analysis

Fundamental analysis focuses on evaluating a company's intrinsic value by examining its financial statements, management, competitive position, and industry conditions. The goal is to determine whether a stock is undervalued or overvalued based on its fundamental characteristics.

To perform fundamental analysis, investors typically look at:

- **Financial Statements:** Key documents include the balance sheet, income statement, and cash flow statement. These documents provide insights into a company's financial health, profitability, and cash generation.

- **Earnings Reports:** Regular earnings reports reveal how well a company is performing. Analysts pay close attention to earnings per share (EPS) and revenue growth.

- **Management:** The quality and track record of a company's management team can significantly impact its success. Strong leadership often correlates with better performance.

- **Industry and Economic Conditions:** Understanding the broader industry context and economic environment helps gauge a company's potential for growth. Factors like market demand, competition, and regulatory changes are considered.

- **Valuation Ratios:** Metrics like the price-to-earnings (P/E) ratio, price-to-book (P/B) ratio, and dividend yield help compare a company's value against its peers and historical performance.

For example, if you're considering investing in a technology company, you might examine its latest financial statements to assess its profitability, check recent earnings reports for revenue trends, evaluate the leadership team's experience, and analyze the competitive landscape. If the company shows strong fundamentals but its stock price is relatively low, it might be considered a good investment opportunity.

Technical Analysis

Technical analysis, on the other hand, involves analyzing statistical trends from trading activity, such as price movements and volume, to predict future stock prices. This method doesn't focus on a company's intrinsic value but rather on patterns and signals that might indicate future price movements.

Key elements of technical analysis include:

- **Price Charts:** Historical price data is plotted on charts to identify patterns and trends. Common chart types include line charts, bar charts, and candlestick charts.

- **Trends and Patterns:** Analysts look for trends (uptrends, downtrends, sideways trends) and patterns (head and shoulders, double tops, triangles) that can signal future movements.

- **Indicators and Oscillators:** Tools like moving averages, relative strength index (RSI), and MACD (moving average convergence divergence) help identify momentum, overbought/oversold conditions, and potential reversals.

- **Support and Resistance Levels:** These are price points where a stock tends to find support as it falls or resistance as it rises. Recognizing these levels helps in making buy or sell decisions.

For instance, if you're looking at a stock's price chart and notice a consistent upward trend with periodic pullbacks to a certain price level (support), you might decide it's a good buying opportunity whenever the stock nears this level.

Choosing Between Fundamental and Technical Analysis

The choice between fundamental and technical analysis depends on your investment style and goals. Fundamental analysis is typically favored by long-term investors who focus on a company's growth potential and intrinsic value. Technical analysis, meanwhile, is often used by short-term traders looking to capitalize on price movements and market trends.

Some investors combine both approaches to get a comprehensive view. They might use fundamental analysis to identify undervalued stocks and technical analysis to determine the best entry and exit points.

For example, a long-term investor might identify a fundamentally strong company that is currently undervalued and then use technical analysis to time their purchase when the stock is showing signs of a price uptrend.

Understanding the differences between fundamental and technical analysis allows you to choose the approach that best suits your investment strategy and helps you make more informed decisions.

Evaluating Companies and Markets

Evaluating companies and markets is a critical skill for making informed investment decisions. Understanding how to analyze both individual companies and broader market trends can help you identify promising investment opportunities and avoid potential pitfalls. This section will guide you through the key aspects of evaluating companies and markets effectively.

Fundamental Analysis of Companies

Fundamental analysis involves assessing a company's financial health, performance, and growth potential. Here are the main components of fundamental analysis:

Financial Statements: Begin by examining a company's financial statements, including the balance sheet, income statement, and cash flow statement. These documents provide insights into the company's financial stability, profitability, and cash management.

Earnings and Revenue: Look at the company's earnings and revenue trends over time. Consistent growth in earnings and revenue is often a sign of a strong and growing business.

Valuation Ratios: Evaluate valuation ratios such as the price-to-earnings (P/E) ratio, price-to-book (P/B) ratio, and price-to-sales (P/S) ratio. These ratios help determine whether a company's stock is fairly valued compared to its earnings, book value, and sales.

Debt Levels: Assess the company's debt levels by looking at the debt-to-equity ratio and interest coverage ratio. High debt levels can be risky, especially if the company struggles to meet its interest payments.

Competitive Position: Consider the company's competitive position within its industry. Companies with strong competitive advantages, such as brand recognition, proprietary technology, or significant market share, are often better positioned for long-term success.

Management Team: Evaluate the quality and track record of the company's management team. Effective leadership can drive a company's growth and navigate challenges successfully.

Qualitative Factors

In addition to quantitative analysis, consider qualitative factors that can impact a company's performance:

Industry Trends: Understand the broader trends and dynamics within the company's industry. Industries with strong growth prospects can provide better opportunities for individual companies.

Market Position: Analyze the company's market position and its ability to adapt to changing market conditions. Companies that can innovate and stay ahead of competitors are more likely to thrive.

Regulatory Environment: Consider the regulatory environment in which the company operates. Regulatory changes can significantly impact a company's operations and profitability.

Evaluating Markets

Evaluating broader market trends is just as important as analyzing individual companies. Here are key factors to consider when assessing markets:

Economic Indicators: Monitor economic indicators such as GDP growth, inflation rates, unemployment rates, and consumer confidence. These indicators provide insights into the overall health of the economy and potential market direction.

Market Trends: Identify market trends by analyzing major stock indices like the S&P 500, NASDAQ, and Dow Jones Industrial Average. Understanding market trends helps you gauge investor sentiment and potential market movements.

Sector Analysis: Different sectors perform differently under various economic conditions. Assessing the performance of different sectors, such as technology, healthcare, finance, and consumer goods, can help you identify which sectors are likely to perform well.

Interest Rates: Keep an eye on interest rate trends set by central banks. Changes in interest rates can affect borrowing costs, consumer spending, and overall economic activity, influencing market performance.

Global Events: Consider the impact of global events, such as geopolitical developments, trade policies, and international economic conditions. Global events can create market volatility and present both risks and opportunities.

Combining Company and Market Analysis

To make well-informed investment decisions, combine your analysis of individual companies with an understanding of broader market trends. This approach allows you to identify strong companies operating in favorable market conditions, enhancing your potential for success.

For example, if you identify a company with solid financials and a strong competitive position in a growing industry, and you also see positive economic indicators and favorable market trends, it might be a good investment opportunity. Conversely, even a strong company might face challenges if the broader market or its industry is experiencing a downturn.

Evaluating companies and markets requires a blend of quantitative analysis, qualitative assessment, and an understanding of broader economic and market trends. By mastering these skills, you can make more informed investment decisions and increase your chances of achieving your financial goals.

Chapter 3: Stock Market Mastery

Understanding Stocks: Types of Stocks

Stocks represent ownership in a company and come in various types, each with its own characteristics and benefits. Understanding the different types of stocks can help you make more informed investment decisions and build a diversified portfolio.

Common Stocks

Common stocks are the most prevalent type of stock that investors buy and sell. When you purchase common stock, you gain ownership in a company and voting rights at shareholder meetings. Common stockholders are entitled to receive dividends, which are portions of the company's profits distributed to shareholders, although these are not guaranteed. The value of common stocks fluctuates based on the company's performance and market conditions, offering potential for both capital gains and losses.

For example, if you invest in a technology company's common stock and the company performs well, the stock price may increase, providing you with capital gains. Additionally, if the company declares dividends, you'll receive a portion of the profits.

Preferred Stocks

Preferred stocks are a type of stock that typically offers fixed dividends, making them similar to bonds. Unlike common stockholders, preferred stockholders usually do not have voting rights. However, they have a higher claim on assets and earnings than common stockholders, meaning they receive dividends before common stockholders and have a higher priority in case of company liquidation.

For instance, if a company is struggling financially but still able to pay dividends, preferred stockholders will receive their fixed dividends first. This makes preferred stocks a more stable income source compared to common stocks, although they generally offer less potential for capital appreciation.

Growth Stocks

Growth stocks belong to companies that are expected to grow at an above-average rate compared to other companies in the market. These companies typically reinvest their earnings into expansion projects, research, and development rather than paying out dividends. Investors buy growth stocks with the expectation that the company's value will increase significantly over time, leading to higher stock prices.

An example of a growth stock might be a startup in the tech industry that is rapidly expanding its market share. Investors purchase shares with the belief that the company's innovative products will drive substantial future growth, resulting in higher stock prices.

Value Stocks

Value stocks are shares of companies that are considered undervalued based on fundamental analysis. These stocks trade at lower prices relative to their earnings, dividends, or other financial metrics. Value investors look for stocks that they believe are being overlooked by the market and have the potential to increase in value as the market recognizes their true worth.

For example, a well-established manufacturing company with a strong track record but currently facing temporary challenges might have its stock priced lower than its intrinsic value. Value investors would see this as an opportunity to buy the stock at a bargain price, expecting it to rise as the company recovers.

Dividend Stocks

Dividend stocks are shares of companies that regularly pay dividends to their shareholders. These stocks are attractive to investors seeking a steady income stream, especially during market volatility. Companies that pay dividends are often well-established with stable earnings.

Consider a utility company that generates consistent profits and distributes a portion of these earnings as dividends. Investors who prioritize income over growth might invest in such dividend-paying stocks to receive regular payments.

Blue-Chip Stocks

Blue-chip stocks represent shares in large, well-established, and financially sound companies with a history of reliable performance. These companies are typically leaders in their industries and are known for their stability, making them attractive to conservative investors.

For instance, investing in a major multinational corporation like a leading consumer goods company offers relative safety and steady returns. Blue-chip stocks might not offer the highest growth potential, but they provide stability and often pay dividends, making them suitable for long-term investment.

Small-Cap, Mid-Cap, and Large-Cap Stocks

Stocks are also categorized based on the company's market capitalization, which is the total market value of its outstanding shares. Small-cap stocks have a market cap of less than $2 billion, mid-cap stocks range from $2 billion to $10 billion, and large-cap stocks exceed $10 billion.

- **Small-Cap Stocks:** These are shares in smaller companies that often offer higher growth potential but come with higher risk and volatility. An example might be a small biotech firm with a promising new drug.

- **Mid-Cap Stocks:** These represent medium-sized companies that balance growth potential and stability. An example could be a regional bank expanding its market reach.

- **Large-Cap Stocks:** These are shares in large, established companies known for stability and reliability. An example would be a major telecommunications company with a global presence.

Understanding the various types of stocks helps you build a diversified portfolio that aligns with your financial goals, risk tolerance, and investment horizon.

How the Stock Market Works

The stock market is a dynamic and complex system that allows investors to buy and sell shares of publicly traded companies. Understanding how the stock market works is essential for anyone looking to invest and grow their wealth. This section will explain the basics of the stock market, how it functions, and the key elements that influence its operations.

The Basics of the Stock Market

At its core, the stock market is a platform where investors can buy and sell ownership stakes in companies, known as stocks or shares. When you purchase a share of a company, you are buying a small piece of that company, making you a shareholder. Shareholders can benefit from the company's success through price appreciation and dividends.

Stock Exchanges

The stock market operates through stock exchanges, which are organized marketplaces where securities are traded. The most well-known stock exchanges include the New York Stock Exchange (NYSE) and the NASDAQ. These exchanges provide a regulated environment that ensures fair trading practices and transparency.

How Stocks are Traded

Stocks are traded through a network of buyers and sellers. When you want to buy or sell a stock, you typically do so through a broker, who acts as an intermediary. Brokers facilitate transactions by matching buyers with sellers, either through traditional stock exchanges or electronic trading platforms.

The price of a stock is determined by supply and demand. If more people want to buy a stock than sell it, the price goes up. Conversely, if more people want to sell a stock than buy it, the price goes down. This constant interaction between buyers and sellers creates the dynamic pricing we see in the stock market.

Initial Public Offerings (IPOs)

Before a company's stock can be traded on a stock exchange, it must go through an initial public offering (IPO). During an IPO, a company sells shares to the public for the first time. This process allows the company to raise capital from investors to fund its operations and growth. Once the IPO is complete, the company's shares are listed on a stock exchange, where they can be traded by the public.

Market Participants

The stock market is made up of various participants, each playing a crucial role in its functioning:

Individual Investors: These are retail investors who buy and sell stocks for their personal investment portfolios. They may trade through online brokerage accounts and seek to build wealth over time.

Institutional Investors: These include entities such as mutual funds, pension funds, hedge funds, and insurance companies. Institutional investors typically manage large sums of money and can influence stock prices through their trading activities.

Market Makers: Market makers are firms or individuals that provide liquidity to the market by buying and selling stocks at publicly quoted prices. They play a crucial role in ensuring there is always a buyer or seller available, which helps stabilize the market.

Regulators: Regulatory bodies, such as the Securities and Exchange Commission (SEC) in the United States, oversee the stock market to ensure it operates fairly and transparently. They enforce rules and regulations designed to protect investors and maintain market integrity.

Stock Market Indices

Stock market indices are tools used to measure and report on the performance of a specific segment of the stock market. Some of the most well-known indices include the Dow Jones Industrial Average (DJIA), the S&P 500, and the NASDAQ Composite. These indices track the performance of a selected group of stocks and provide a snapshot of how the market or a particular sector is performing.

Factors Influencing the Stock Market

Several factors can influence the stock market's performance:

Economic Indicators: Indicators such as GDP growth, employment rates, and consumer spending can impact investor sentiment and market performance. Positive economic data often boosts market confidence, while negative data can lead to declines.

Corporate Performance: The financial health and performance of individual companies play a significant role in their stock prices. Strong earnings reports, new product launches, and strategic acquisitions can drive stock prices up, while poor performance can lead to declines.

Interest Rates: Central banks, such as the Federal Reserve in the United States, influence the stock market through their control of interest rates. Lower interest rates tend to boost the market by making borrowing cheaper and encouraging investment, while higher rates can have the opposite effect.

Global Events: Events such as geopolitical developments, natural disasters, and global pandemics can create uncertainty and volatility in the stock market. Investors often react to these events by buying or selling stocks based on perceived risks and opportunities.

The Role of Technology

Technology has revolutionized the stock market, making it more accessible to individual investors and increasing the speed and efficiency of trading. Online brokerage platforms and mobile apps have made it easier than ever for people to buy and sell stocks. Additionally, algorithmic trading and high-frequency trading have introduced new dynamics to the market, allowing for rapid execution of trades and increased market liquidity.

Understanding how the stock market works is fundamental to becoming a successful investor. By grasping the basic principles of stock trading, the role of various market participants, and the factors that influence stock prices, you can make more informed investment decisions and navigate the market with greater confidence.

Trading Procedure on a Stock Exchange. Source: geeksforgeeks.org

Strategies for Stock Investment: Growth Investing

Growth investing is an investment strategy focused on buying shares in companies that are expected to grow at an above-average rate compared to other companies. The goal is to profit from the increase in the stock price as the company grows. This strategy is often chosen by investors looking for significant capital appreciation rather than immediate income from dividends.

Characteristics of Growth Companies

Growth companies are typically in industries that are expanding rapidly, such as technology, healthcare, and consumer discretionary sectors. These companies often reinvest their earnings into the business to fuel further growth, rather than paying out dividends to shareholders. As a result, they usually exhibit high revenue growth rates and potential for substantial earnings increases.

For example, a tech startup developing innovative software solutions might be considered a growth company. If the company's products gain market acceptance, it could experience rapid revenue and profit growth, leading to a higher stock price.

Evaluating Growth Stocks

When evaluating potential growth stocks, investors look at several key factors. One of the most important is revenue growth. Companies with consistently high revenue growth rates are often seen as good growth candidates. Additionally, investors examine earnings growth, profit margins, and return on equity (ROE). These metrics provide insight into the company's profitability and efficiency in generating returns from shareholders' equity.

It's also crucial to consider the company's market potential. Companies operating in expanding markets or those with unique products and services that address unmet needs tend to offer better growth prospects. The competitive landscape is another important consideration. Companies with a competitive edge, such as a strong brand, proprietary technology, or high barriers to entry, are more likely to sustain their growth.

Risks of Growth Investing

While growth investing can offer substantial rewards, it also comes with higher risks. Growth stocks are often more volatile than other stocks, meaning their prices can fluctuate widely in the short term. This volatility can be driven by high investor expectations, which can lead to significant price drops if the company fails to meet these expectations.

Furthermore, growth companies often reinvest profits back into the business rather than paying dividends. This can make them less attractive to investors seeking steady income. Additionally, growth stocks can be more susceptible to economic downturns. In challenging economic conditions, companies with high growth rates might struggle to maintain their performance.

Examples of Growth Stocks

Consider a company like Tesla, which has shown remarkable growth over the past decade. Tesla's focus on electric vehicles and renewable energy solutions has positioned it as a leader in the industry. Despite its high valuation, investors continue to buy Tesla stock based on its potential for future growth and market expansion.

Another example is a tech giant like Amazon. Over the years, Amazon has expanded from an online bookstore to a global e-commerce leader, cloud computing provider, and more. Its aggressive reinvestment strategy and continuous innovation have fueled its growth, making it a favorite among growth investors.

Implementing a Growth Investing Strategy

To implement a growth investing strategy, it's important to conduct thorough research and stay informed about the companies and industries you're investing in. This involves reading financial reports, staying updated on industry trends, and monitoring the company's performance.

Diversification is also key. While it's tempting to concentrate on a few high-potential growth stocks, spreading your investments across different sectors and companies can help mitigate risk. It's also essential to have a long-term perspective. Growth investing often requires patience, as it can take time for companies to realize their full growth potential.

Investors should regularly review their portfolios to ensure that the companies they have invested in continue to meet their growth criteria. Adjustments may be necessary if a company's growth prospects change or if better opportunities arise.

Growth investing is a dynamic and potentially rewarding strategy that can significantly enhance your portfolio's performance. By focusing on companies with high growth potential, you can benefit from the capital appreciation that comes with their success. However, it's important to stay mindful of the risks and be prepared for the volatility that often accompanies growth stocks.

Value Investing

Value investing is a strategy that involves picking stocks that appear to be trading for less than their intrinsic or book value. Investors who use this strategy believe that the market overreacts to good and bad news, resulting in stock price movements that do not correspond with a company's long-term fundamentals. The result is an opportunity to profit by buying undervalued stocks.

The Philosophy Behind Value Investing

The core philosophy of value investing is that the stock market is not always efficient, and sometimes stocks are mispriced. Value investors seek to capitalize on these inefficiencies. They look for stocks that are undervalued by the market, believing that these stocks will eventually be recognized for their true worth, leading to price appreciation.

Identifying Undervalued Stocks

Value investors use several criteria to identify undervalued stocks:

Price-to-Earnings (P/E) Ratio: This ratio compares a company's share price to its earnings per share. A low P/E ratio might indicate that the stock is undervalued relative to its earnings.

Price-to-Book (P/B) Ratio: This ratio compares a company's market value to its book value. A P/B ratio less than one could suggest that the stock is undervalued relative to the company's assets.

Dividend Yield: Value investors may look for stocks with high dividend yields, as this can indicate a company is generating sufficient cash flow to return money to shareholders, potentially signaling that the stock is undervalued.

Debt Levels: Evaluating a company's debt levels is crucial. Companies with manageable debt levels are often considered less risky and more attractive to value investors.

Cash Flow: Strong, consistent cash flow is a sign of a healthy company. Value investors often seek companies with solid cash flow that are temporarily undervalued by the market.

The Margin of Safety

A key concept in value investing is the margin of safety. This principle involves buying stocks at a significant discount to their intrinsic value, providing a cushion against errors in analysis or unforeseen events. The margin of safety reduces the risk of losing money and increases the potential for higher returns.

Long-Term Perspective

Value investing requires patience and a long-term perspective. Value investors are not swayed by short-term market fluctuations or popular trends. Instead, they focus on the underlying fundamentals of the companies they invest in, confident that the market will eventually recognize and correct the stock's undervaluation.

Famous Value Investors

Several renowned investors have successfully applied the value investing approach. Benjamin Graham, known as the "father of value investing," laid the foundation for this strategy with his book "The Intelligent Investor." Warren Buffett, a student of Graham, has also famously utilized value investing principles to build his fortune, emphasizing the importance of buying quality companies at fair prices and holding them for the long term.

Challenges of Value Investing

Despite its potential rewards, value investing is not without challenges. Identifying undervalued stocks requires thorough research and analysis, and there is always the risk that the market may take longer than expected to recognize a stock's true value. Additionally, value stocks can remain undervalued for extended periods, testing the patience of investors.

Tools and Resources

Value investors often rely on various tools and resources to aid their research and decision-making processes. Financial statements, annual reports, and SEC filings provide critical insights into a company's operations and financial health. Screening tools and financial news platforms can help identify potential value stocks and stay updated on market developments.

Value investing is a disciplined and patient approach that seeks to exploit market inefficiencies by buying undervalued stocks. While it requires significant research and a long-term perspective, the rewards can be substantial for those who are diligent and committed to the principles of value investing. This strategy emphasizes the importance of sound analysis, a margin of safety, and a focus on fundamental value over market trends.

Advanced Stock Market Techniques: Options and Futures

Options and futures are advanced financial instruments that investors use to manage risk, speculate on future price movements, or enhance their portfolios. While they can be complex and risky, understanding how they work can open up new strategies for experienced investors.

Options

An option is a contract that gives the holder the right, but not the obligation, to buy or sell an asset at a predetermined price before or on a specified date. There are two main types of options: call options and put options.

- **Call Options:** These give the holder the right to buy an asset at a specified price (the strike price) within a set time period. Investors purchase call options if they expect the price of the underlying asset to rise. For example, if you buy a call option for a stock at a strike price of $50 and the stock rises to $60, you can buy the stock at $50 and potentially sell it at $60, profiting from the difference.

- **Put Options:** These give the holder the right to sell an asset at a specified price within a set time period. Investors buy put options if they expect the price of the underlying asset to fall. For instance, if you buy a put option for a stock at a strike price of $50 and the stock drops to $40, you can sell the stock at $50, thus profiting from the price decline.

Options can be used for various strategies, such as hedging against potential losses in a portfolio, generating income through selling options, or speculating on market movements with a limited risk of loss.

Futures

Futures contracts are agreements to buy or sell an asset at a future date for a price agreed upon today. Unlike options, futures contracts obligate the buyer to purchase, and the seller to sell, the underlying asset at the contract's expiration.

Futures are commonly used in commodities markets for items like oil, gold, and agricultural products, but they can also be applied to financial instruments like currencies and stock indices.

For example, an airline company might buy oil futures to lock in current prices and protect against future price increases. If oil prices rise, the company benefits from having secured a lower price. Conversely, if prices fall, they are still obligated to buy at the higher, agreed-upon price, which can result in a loss.

Leverage and Margin

Both options and futures often involve leverage, allowing investors to control a large position with a relatively small amount of capital. This can amplify both gains and losses. For instance, with options, you might pay a small premium to control a larger amount of the underlying asset. In futures trading, a small margin deposit can control a substantial contract value.

However, leverage increases risk. If the market moves against your position, you could face significant losses, potentially exceeding your initial investment. Therefore, it's crucial to manage risk carefully when using leverage.

Hedging and Speculation

One primary use of options and futures is hedging, which involves taking a position in these instruments to offset potential losses in another investment. For example, if you own a portfolio of stocks, you might buy put options to protect against a market downturn.

Speculation involves taking positions in options or futures based on expectations of future price movements, aiming to profit from those movements. This can be highly risky, as it requires accurate predictions about market directions.

Risks and Considerations

Options and futures are not suitable for all investors. They require a thorough understanding of the market, the underlying assets, and the mechanics of the contracts. Potential risks include market volatility, leverage-induced losses, and the complexity of predicting price movements.

Before engaging in options or futures trading, it's advisable to gain experience with less risky investments and to consult with financial professionals. Many investors also benefit from using paper trading accounts to practice strategies without risking real money.

Understanding and effectively using options and futures can add valuable tools to your investment strategy. These instruments offer unique opportunities for hedging and speculation, but they also come with significant risks that require careful management and a solid understanding of market dynamics.

Short Selling

Short selling is an investment strategy that allows investors to profit from a decline in a stock's price. Unlike traditional investing, where you buy a stock with the hope that its price will rise, short selling involves borrowing shares of a stock and selling them with the expectation that the price will drop. When the price falls, you buy back the shares at the lower price, return them to the lender, and pocket the difference as profit.

How Short Selling Works

To engage in short selling, you follow a few key steps:

1. **Borrowing Shares**: First, you borrow shares of the stock from a broker. These shares come from the broker's own inventory, another client, or a third party.

2. **Selling the Shares**: Once you have borrowed the shares, you sell them on the open market at the current market price. This creates a short position.

3. **Waiting for the Price to Drop**: After selling the shares, you wait for the stock price to decline. The goal is for the

stock price to drop significantly below the price at which you sold the borrowed shares.

4. **Buying Back the Shares**: When the stock price has fallen to your target level, you buy back the same number of shares you initially borrowed. This process is known as covering your short position.

5. **Returning the Shares**: Finally, you return the borrowed shares to the broker. The difference between the price at which you sold the shares and the price at which you bought them back represents your profit, minus any interest or fees charged by the broker for borrowing the shares.

Risks of Short Selling

Short selling carries significant risks and is considered a high-risk strategy. One of the primary risks is the potential for unlimited losses. Unlike traditional stock purchases, where the maximum loss is the amount invested, short selling can result in losses that exceed the initial investment. This happens because there is no limit to how high a stock's price can rise.

For example, if you short sell a stock at $50 per share and the price increases to $100, you would need to buy back the shares at the higher price, resulting in a substantial loss. In extreme cases, a rapidly rising stock price can lead to margin calls, where the broker demands additional funds to cover potential losses.

Short Squeezes

A short squeeze occurs when a heavily shorted stock's price begins to rise rapidly, forcing short sellers to buy back shares to limit their losses. This buying activity can drive the stock price even higher, creating a feedback loop that exacerbates the price increase. Short squeezes can lead to significant losses for short sellers and are a major risk associated with this strategy.

Benefits of Short Selling

Despite its risks, short selling can offer several benefits:

- **Hedging**: Investors can use short selling to hedge against potential losses in their long positions. For instance, if you own shares of a company but are concerned about a short-term decline, you can short sell another stock in the same industry to offset potential losses.

- **Market Efficiency**: Short selling contributes to market efficiency by allowing investors to profit from overvalued stocks. This can help correct mispricings in the market and bring stock prices closer to their true value.

- **Profit Opportunities**: Short selling provides an opportunity to profit in declining markets. This can be particularly useful during bear markets or periods of economic downturn when stock prices are falling.

Regulations and Restrictions

Short selling is subject to various regulations and restrictions designed to prevent market manipulation and excessive risk-taking. In many markets, regulators impose rules such as the uptick rule, which allows short selling only when the last sale price was higher than the previous price. Additionally, brokers may have their own requirements and restrictions on short selling, including margin requirements and borrowing fees.

Strategies for Short Selling

Successful short selling requires careful analysis and a thorough understanding of the market. Investors often use technical analysis, financial statement analysis, and market sentiment indicators to identify potential short-selling opportunities. It is also crucial to have a well-defined exit strategy to limit losses and lock in profits.

Short selling is a sophisticated investment strategy that allows investors to profit from declining stock prices. While it offers the potential for significant gains, it also carries substantial risks, including the possibility of unlimited losses and short squeezes. As such, short selling should be approached with caution and a thorough understanding of the market dynamics.

Chapter 4: Fixed Income and Bonds

Basics of Bonds: What are Bonds?

Bonds are debt securities issued by governments, municipalities, or corporations to raise capital. When you buy a bond, you are essentially lending money to the issuer in exchange for regular interest payments and the return of the bond's face value, or principal, when it matures.

How Bonds Work

When an entity needs to raise funds, it can issue bonds to investors. Each bond has a face value, which is the amount the issuer agrees to repay the bondholder at the end of the bond's term, known as the maturity date. Bonds also come with a fixed interest rate, called the coupon rate, which determines the regular interest payments made to bondholders, usually semi-annually or annually.

For example, if you purchase a bond with a face value of $1,000 and a coupon rate of 5%, you will receive $50 in interest payments each year until the bond matures. At maturity, you will also get back the $1,000 principal.

Types of Bonds

There are several types of bonds, each with its own characteristics and risk levels.

Government Bonds

Government bonds are issued by national governments and are considered among the safest investments because they are backed by the government's credit. In the United States, these are known as Treasury bonds (T-bonds). Other countries have similar bonds, such as gilts in the UK or JGBs (Japanese Government Bonds) in Japan.

Municipal Bonds

Municipal bonds, or munis, are issued by state and local governments or their agencies. These bonds are often used to fund public projects like schools, highways, and water systems. One key advantage of municipal bonds is that their interest payments are often exempt from federal income taxes and, in some cases, state and local taxes as well.

Corporate Bonds

Corporate bonds are issued by companies to raise capital for business activities, such as expanding operations or funding new projects. These bonds typically offer higher interest rates than government or municipal bonds due to the higher risk of default. Corporate bonds are graded by credit rating agencies based on the issuing company's financial stability and creditworthiness.

Zero-Coupon Bonds

Zero-coupon bonds do not pay regular interest. Instead, they are sold at a discount to their face value and mature at full face value. The difference between the purchase price and the face value represents the bondholder's return. For example, you might buy a zero-coupon bond for $800 that matures at $1,000 in 10 years. The $200 difference is your interest earned over the bond's term.

How Bonds Are Traded

Bonds can be bought and sold in the secondary market after they are issued. Their prices fluctuate based on interest rates, economic conditions, and the issuer's creditworthiness. When interest rates rise, bond prices generally fall, and vice versa. This inverse relationship occurs because new bonds are issued at current higher rates, making existing bonds with lower rates less attractive.

Benefits of Investing in Bonds

Bonds are often included in investment portfolios for their stability and income generation. They are generally less volatile than stocks and can provide a steady stream of income through interest payments. Additionally, because bonds have a set maturity date and principal repayment, they can help preserve capital.

For instance, if you are nearing retirement and seek to protect your savings, adding bonds to your portfolio can provide a more predictable return and reduce overall risk.

Risks Associated with Bonds

Despite their stability, bonds are not risk-free. Interest rate risk is the most significant, as rising interest rates can decrease the market value of existing bonds. There is also credit risk, which is the possibility that the issuer may default on interest payments or fail to repay the principal. Inflation risk is another consideration, as rising inflation can erode the purchasing power of the fixed interest payments over time.

By understanding the fundamentals of bonds, including how they work, their types, and the associated risks, you can make informed decisions and effectively incorporate bonds into your investment strategy. This knowledge helps you balance your portfolio, manage risk, and achieve your financial goals.

Types of Bonds

Bonds are a type of debt security that allow investors to lend money to issuers in exchange for periodic interest payments and the return of the principal amount at maturity. Bonds can be issued by governments, municipalities, corporations, and other entities. Understanding the different types of bonds available can help you make informed investment decisions that align with your financial goals and risk tolerance.

Government Bonds

Government bonds are issued by national governments and are considered one of the safest types of investments. These bonds are backed by the government's credit, making them low-risk. Common types of government bonds include:

Treasury Bonds: Issued by the U.S. Department of the Treasury, these bonds have maturities ranging from 10 to 30 years. They pay interest semiannually and are backed by the full faith and credit of the U.S. government.

Treasury Notes: Also issued by the U.S. Treasury, these bonds have shorter maturities, typically ranging from 2 to 10 years. Like Treasury bonds, they pay interest semiannually.

Treasury Bills: These are short-term securities with maturities of one year or less. Treasury bills are sold at a discount to their face value, and investors receive the face value at maturity. The difference between the purchase price and the face value represents the interest earned.

Municipal Bonds: Issued by state and local governments, municipal bonds (or "munis") are used to fund public projects such as schools, highways, and water systems. The interest earned on municipal bonds is often exempt from federal income tax and, in some cases, state and local taxes as well.

Corporate Bonds

Corporate bonds are issued by companies to raise capital for various purposes, such as expanding operations or funding new projects. These bonds typically offer higher yields than government bonds to compensate for the increased risk. Corporate bonds can be categorized into two main types:

Investment-Grade Bonds: These bonds are issued by companies with strong credit ratings, indicating a low risk of default. Investment-grade bonds offer lower yields compared to higher-risk bonds but provide more stability and reliability.

High-Yield Bonds: Also known as "junk bonds," these are issued by companies with lower credit ratings. High-yield bonds offer higher interest rates to compensate for the increased risk of default. While they can provide attractive returns, they also carry a higher level of risk.

Agency Bonds

Agency bonds are issued by government-sponsored enterprises (GSEs) or federal agencies to support specific sectors of the economy, such as housing or agriculture. Examples of agency bonds include those issued by the Federal National Mortgage Association (Fannie Mae) and the Federal Home Loan Mortgage Corporation (Freddie Mac). These bonds often provide slightly higher yields than Treasury bonds but are still considered relatively safe.

International Bonds

International bonds are issued by foreign governments or corporations. Investing in international bonds allows investors to diversify their portfolios and gain exposure to different economic conditions and interest rate environments. However, international bonds also come with additional risks, such as currency risk and political risk.

Convertible Bonds

Convertible bonds are a type of corporate bond that can be converted into a predetermined number of the issuing company's shares. This feature provides the potential for capital appreciation if the company's stock price increases. Convertible bonds typically offer lower interest rates than regular corporate bonds due to the added benefit of conversion.

Zero-Coupon Bonds

Zero-coupon bonds do not pay periodic interest. Instead, they are sold at a deep discount to their face value and mature at their face value. The difference between the purchase price and the face value represents the investor's return. Zero-coupon bonds can be issued by governments or corporations and are suitable for investors who do not need regular income but are looking for a lump sum payment at maturity.

Floating Rate Bonds

Floating rate bonds, also known as variable rate bonds, have interest payments that fluctuate with changes in market interest rates. The interest rate is typically tied to a benchmark rate, such as the LIBOR or the federal funds rate. Floating rate bonds can provide protection against rising interest rates, as their yields adjust upward with increasing rates.

Bonds are a diverse category of investments, each with unique features, benefits, and risks. Whether you are looking for safety, higher yields, or diversification, understanding the different types of bonds can help you build a balanced and effective investment portfolio.

Investing in Bonds: Bond Ratings and What They Mean

Bond ratings are assessments of the creditworthiness of bond issuers, provided by rating agencies. These ratings give investors an idea of the risk associated with a bond, specifically the likelihood that the issuer will be able to meet its financial obligations, including paying interest and repaying the principal. Understanding bond ratings can help investors make informed decisions about which bonds to include in their portfolios.

Major Rating Agencies

The three primary rating agencies are Moody's, Standard & Poor's (S&P), and Fitch. Each agency uses its own rating scale to evaluate the credit risk of bonds.

Rating Scales

The ratings range from high-grade, indicating low credit risk, to junk bonds, indicating higher credit risk. Here's a simplified version of the rating scales:

- **Moody's:** Aaa, Aa, A, Baa, Ba, B, Caa, Ca, C
- **S&P and Fitch:** AAA, AA, A, BBB, BB, B, CCC, CC, C, D

Bonds rated Baa3 or higher by Moody's, or BBB- or higher by S&P and Fitch, are considered investment-grade. Bonds below these ratings are considered non-investment grade or high-yield (often referred to as junk bonds).

Investment-Grade Bonds

Investment-grade bonds are issued by entities with a strong capacity to meet their financial commitments. These bonds are considered safer and less likely to default. Governments and financially stable corporations typically issue investment-grade bonds. They offer lower yields compared to high-yield bonds but provide more security.

For example, a U.S. Treasury bond is considered one of the safest investments and typically receives the highest rating (AAA or Aaa), reflecting its low risk of default.

High-Yield (Junk) Bonds

High-yield bonds are issued by entities with a higher risk of default. These bonds offer higher interest rates to compensate investors for the increased risk. Companies with weaker financial stability or those operating in volatile industries often issue high-yield bonds.

While high-yield bonds can enhance returns in a diversified portfolio, they also come with greater risk. For instance, a startup company with uncertain future prospects might issue high-yield bonds to attract investors willing to take on more risk for potentially higher returns.

Downgrades and Upgrades

Bond ratings are not static and can be upgraded or downgraded based on the issuer's financial health and economic conditions. A downgrade indicates increased risk, which can lead to a decrease in the bond's market value. Conversely, an upgrade suggests improved financial stability, potentially increasing the bond's value.

For example, if a company's financial situation worsens, Moody's might downgrade its bond rating from Baa to Ba, signaling increased risk. This downgrade often results in a drop in the bond's price as investors seek to sell off riskier investments.

Importance of Bond Ratings

Bond ratings provide a useful benchmark for investors, helping them assess the risk and make informed decisions. Ratings allow investors to compare bonds from different issuers and industries on a standardized scale. However, it's important to remember that ratings are not infallible and should be one of several factors considered when evaluating a bond.

Investors should also consider their own risk tolerance, investment goals, and market conditions. For instance, a conservative investor might prefer sticking to high-rated, investment-grade bonds, while an investor seeking higher returns might allocate a portion of their portfolio to high-yield bonds, accepting the increased risk.

Due Diligence

Even with bond ratings, it's crucial for investors to perform their own due diligence. This includes understanding the issuer's financial health, the economic environment, and how interest rate changes might impact bond prices. Regularly reviewing bond ratings and staying informed about market trends can help investors manage risk and optimize their bond investments.

Bond ratings are a vital tool for assessing the risk associated with bond investments. They help investors understand the creditworthiness of issuers and make more informed decisions, balancing risk and return to achieve their financial objectives.

Strategies for Bond Investment

Investing in bonds can provide a steady income stream, preserve capital, and diversify your investment portfolio. However, like any investment, successful bond investing requires strategic planning and a good understanding of how different bonds and market conditions interact. Here are several strategies to help you make the most of your bond investments.

Laddering

Bond laddering involves purchasing bonds with different maturities. This strategy helps manage interest rate risk and provides regular income. By staggering maturities, you ensure that a portion of your portfolio is maturing regularly, giving you the opportunity to reinvest at current interest rates. For example, you might buy bonds maturing in one, three, five, and ten years. As each bond matures, you reinvest the proceeds in new bonds with longer maturities, maintaining the ladder.

Barbell Strategy

The barbell strategy focuses on investing in short-term and long-term bonds while avoiding intermediate maturities. This approach aims to balance the higher yields of long-term bonds with the liquidity and lower risk of short-term bonds. For instance, you might invest half of your portfolio in bonds maturing within one to three years and the other half in bonds maturing in ten to twenty years. This diversification can help mitigate the risks associated with interest rate fluctuations.

Bullet Strategy

The bullet strategy involves investing in bonds that all mature at the same time. This approach is useful if you have a specific financial goal in mind, such as funding a child's education or purchasing a home, and you want to ensure that your investments mature when you need the money. By aligning all your bond maturities with your target date, you can plan for a lump sum payment at a specific point in time.

Interest Rate Anticipation

This strategy involves adjusting your bond portfolio based on expected changes in interest rates. If you anticipate that interest rates will rise, you might reduce your exposure to long-term bonds, which are more sensitive to interest rate changes, and increase your holdings of short-term bonds or floating-rate bonds. Conversely, if you expect interest rates to fall, you might invest more in long-term bonds to lock in higher yields.

Credit Quality Diversification

Diversifying by credit quality involves investing in bonds with varying credit ratings to balance risk and return. High-quality bonds (e.g., government and investment-grade corporate bonds) offer lower yields but greater safety, while lower-quality bonds (e.g., high-yield or junk bonds) offer higher yields but carry more risk. By holding a mix of bonds with different credit ratings, you can achieve a balance between income and risk.

Sector Diversification

Just as you diversify across asset classes, diversifying across different sectors can reduce risk and enhance returns. Bonds are issued by various sectors, including government, corporate, municipal, and international entities. Investing across these sectors helps mitigate the impact of sector-specific risks and provides exposure to different economic conditions.

Reinvestment Strategy

A reinvestment strategy involves using the interest income generated by your bond portfolio to purchase additional bonds. This can help compound your returns over time. For example, if you receive interest payments from a bond, you can reinvest those payments into new bonds, gradually increasing your portfolio's size and income-generating potential.

Inflation Protection

To protect against inflation, consider including inflation-protected securities in your bond portfolio. Treasury Inflation-Protected Securities (TIPS) are government bonds that adjust their principal value based on inflation, as measured by the Consumer Price Index (CPI). These bonds can help preserve your purchasing power by providing returns that keep pace with inflation.

Active Bond Management

Active bond management involves regularly monitoring and adjusting your bond portfolio based on changing market conditions and investment goals. This strategy can include buying and selling bonds to capitalize on interest rate movements, credit rating changes, or economic forecasts. Active management requires a more hands-on approach and a deeper understanding of the bond market.

Buy and Hold

The buy-and-hold strategy is a passive approach where you purchase bonds and hold them until maturity. This strategy is straightforward and minimizes transaction costs. By holding bonds to maturity, you avoid interest rate risk and ensure that you receive the bond's face value at maturity, along with periodic interest payments.

Successful bond investing involves a combination of strategies tailored to your financial goals, risk tolerance, and market outlook. Whether you choose laddering, a barbell approach, or active management, understanding these strategies can help you build a robust bond portfolio that meets your income and growth objectives.

Managing Bond Investments: Yield Curve Analysis

Yield curve analysis is a valuable tool for bond investors, providing insights into interest rate trends, economic expectations, and potential investment opportunities. The yield curve plots the interest rates of bonds with equal credit quality but differing maturity dates, typically from three months to 30 years.

What is the Yield Curve?

The yield curve is a graphical representation showing the relationship between bond yields and their maturities. Typically, the curve is constructed using U.S. Treasury securities because they are considered risk-free benchmarks.

The yield curve can take various shapes, each offering different insights into market conditions and investor expectations:

- **Normal Yield Curve:** This upward-sloping curve indicates that longer-term bonds have higher yields than shorter-term bonds. It suggests that investors expect steady economic growth and higher future interest rates.

- **Inverted Yield Curve:** An inverted curve slopes downward, meaning short-term yields are higher than long-term yields. This unusual situation often signals investor concerns about future economic decline or recession.

- **Flat Yield Curve:** A flat curve occurs when short-term and long-term yields are very close. This can indicate economic uncertainty or a transition period between economic growth and recession.

Why Analyze the Yield Curve?

Yield curve analysis helps investors make informed decisions about bond investments and broader economic conditions.

Economic Indicators

The shape of the yield curve is a powerful economic indicator. A normal yield curve suggests positive economic growth and stable inflation, which are conducive to higher future interest rates. An inverted yield curve has historically preceded recessions, as it reflects market expectations of declining interest rates due to economic slowdowns. A flat yield curve can indicate uncertainty or a period of economic transition.

Interest Rate Expectations

The yield curve reflects market expectations for future interest rates. If the curve steepens, it suggests that investors expect higher future interest rates due to anticipated economic growth or rising inflation. Conversely, a flattening or inverted curve suggests expectations of lower future rates, possibly due to economic contraction or deflationary pressures.

Investment Strategy

Investors use yield curve analysis to inform their bond investment strategies. For example, in a normal yield curve environment, investors might prefer long-term bonds to lock in higher yields. In an inverted curve scenario, they might favor short-term bonds, anticipating lower future rates and the possibility of reinvesting at higher yields when the curve normalizes.

Risk Management

The yield curve also helps in assessing the risk of holding different maturities. Long-term bonds are more sensitive to interest rate changes, known as interest rate risk. When the yield curve is steep, the potential reward for taking on this risk is higher. Conversely, when the curve is flat or inverted, the additional yield for long-term bonds is minimal, suggesting higher relative risk for little additional return.

Practical Example of Yield Curve Analysis

Consider a situation where the yield curve is steepening. This steepening indicates that long-term interest rates are rising faster than short-term rates. An investor might interpret this as a signal of future economic growth and potential inflation. In response, they might increase their holdings in long-term bonds to benefit from higher yields, expecting that the overall economic environment will remain favorable.

Alternatively, if the yield curve is flattening or inverting, an investor might become more cautious. They might shift their focus to short-term bonds or even high-quality, shorter-duration investments to reduce exposure to potential economic downturns and lower future interest rates.

Interpreting Changes in the Yield Curve

Monitoring changes in the yield curve over time can provide ongoing insights into market sentiment and economic conditions. For example, a sudden shift from a normal to a flat or inverted curve could prompt a reassessment of risk exposure and investment strategy. Investors might seek to understand the underlying factors driving these changes, such as shifts in Federal Reserve policy, inflation expectations, or global economic events.

Yield curve analysis is a crucial component of bond investing, offering insights into interest rate trends, economic expectations, and potential investment strategies. By understanding and interpreting the yield curve, investors can make more informed decisions, manage risks effectively, and optimize their bond portfolios in various economic environments.

Bond Laddering

Bond laddering is a strategy designed to manage interest rate risk and provide a steady income stream. This approach involves purchasing multiple bonds with staggered maturities. As each bond matures, the proceeds are reinvested in a new bond with a longer maturity, maintaining the ladder structure. This method offers several benefits, including reduced interest rate risk, liquidity, and the potential for higher returns over time.

How Bond Laddering Works

Imagine you have $50,000 to invest in bonds. Instead of investing the entire amount in a single bond, you divide it into five equal parts and purchase five bonds, each with a different maturity date. For example:

- $10,000 in a 1-year bond
- $10,000 in a 2-year bond
- $10,000 in a 3-year bond

- $10,000 in a 4-year bond

- $10,000 in a 5-year bond

As the 1-year bond matures, you reinvest the proceeds into a new 5-year bond. The next year, the 2-year bond matures, and you again reinvest in a new 5-year bond. This process continues, creating a ladder where a portion of your investment matures each year, providing regular income and opportunities to adjust your portfolio based on current interest rates.

Benefits of Bond Laddering

Reduced Interest Rate Risk: One of the primary advantages of bond laddering is that it helps mitigate interest rate risk. When interest rates rise, the value of existing bonds typically falls. However, with a ladder, only a portion of your portfolio is exposed to interest rate fluctuations at any given time. This reduces the overall impact on your investment.

Steady Income Stream: Bond laddering ensures a regular income stream, as bonds mature periodically. This can be particularly beneficial for retirees or those needing a predictable cash flow. The periodic maturity of bonds provides opportunities to access cash without having to sell bonds before maturity, which could result in losses if market conditions are unfavorable.

Flexibility and Liquidity: As bonds in the ladder mature regularly, you have the flexibility to reinvest the proceeds based on current market conditions. This allows you to take advantage of higher interest rates when they occur. Additionally, the regular maturity dates provide liquidity, enabling you to adjust your investment strategy as needed.

Diversification: By investing in bonds with different maturities, you diversify your portfolio. This diversification helps spread risk and reduces the impact of any single bond's performance on your overall portfolio. It also allows you to balance the higher yields of long-term bonds with the stability and lower risk of short-term bonds.

Implementing a Bond Ladder

To implement a bond ladder, follow these steps:

1. **Determine Your Investment Amount**: Decide how much money you want to allocate to your bond ladder.

2. **Choose the Ladder Length**: Select the range of maturities for your bonds. Common ladder lengths range from five to ten years, but you can adjust this based on your financial goals and market conditions.

3. **Select Bonds**: Choose bonds with varying maturities within your selected range. Ensure that the bonds are of high quality to minimize default risk. You can opt for government bonds, municipal bonds, or high-quality corporate bonds, depending on your risk tolerance and investment objectives.

4. **Purchase Bonds**: Buy the bonds and establish your ladder. Allocate equal amounts to each maturity to create a balanced ladder.

5. **Reinvest Proceeds**: As bonds mature, reinvest the proceeds into new bonds with the longest maturity in your ladder. This maintains the ladder's structure and ensures continuous income and risk management.

Example of a Bond Ladder

Suppose you have $100,000 and want to create a 5-year bond ladder. You could allocate $20,000 to each of the following maturities:

- $20,000 in a 1-year bond
- $20,000 in a 2-year bond
- $20,000 in a 3-year bond

- $20,000 in a 4-year bond

- $20,000 in a 5-year bond

When the 1-year bond matures, reinvest the $20,000 in a new 5-year bond. The next year, reinvest the proceeds from the maturing 2-year bond into another 5-year bond. This process continues, maintaining the ladder and providing regular opportunities to adjust your portfolio.

Bond laddering is a practical and effective strategy for managing interest rate risk, ensuring liquidity, and providing a steady income stream. By diversifying maturities and regularly reinvesting proceeds, you can build a resilient bond portfolio that adapts to changing market conditions and aligns with your financial goals.

Chapter 5: Mutual Funds and ETFs

Understanding Mutual Funds: Types of Mutual Funds

Mutual funds are investment vehicles that pool money from many investors to purchase a diversified portfolio of stocks, bonds, or other securities. They are managed by professional portfolio managers and offer investors an easy way to diversify their holdings. Understanding the different types of mutual funds can help you choose the right ones for your investment goals and risk tolerance.

Equity Funds

Equity funds, also known as stock funds, invest primarily in stocks. They aim to generate high returns through capital appreciation, dividends, or both. Equity funds can be further categorized based on the size of the companies they invest in (large-cap, mid-cap, or small-cap), the investment style (growth, value, or blend), and geographic focus (domestic or international).

For example, a large-cap growth fund invests in large companies with strong growth potential, while an international equity fund focuses on stocks of companies outside the investor's home country.

Bond Funds

Bond funds invest in bonds and other fixed-income securities. These funds are designed to provide regular income through interest payments and to preserve capital. Bond funds can vary widely based on the types of bonds they hold, such as government bonds, corporate bonds, municipal bonds, or high-yield (junk) bonds.

An investor looking for stable income might choose a government bond fund, while someone seeking higher returns might opt for a high-yield bond fund, despite the increased risk.

Money Market Funds

Money market funds invest in short-term, high-quality debt securities like Treasury bills, commercial paper, and certificates of deposit. These funds are considered very low risk and aim to provide a stable share price with modest returns. They are ideal for investors looking for a safe place to park their cash temporarily.

For instance, if you have funds you might need in the near future but still want to earn some interest, a money market fund could be a suitable option.

Balanced Funds

Balanced funds, also known as hybrid funds, invest in a mix of stocks and bonds to provide both growth and income. The allocation between stocks and bonds can vary depending on the fund's objective. These funds are designed to offer moderate growth with lower volatility compared to pure equity funds.

A typical balanced fund might hold 60% stocks and 40% bonds, providing a blend of growth and income that can appeal to investors seeking a middle-ground approach.

Index Funds

Index funds aim to replicate the performance of a specific market index, such as the S&P 500 or the Dow Jones Industrial Average. These funds passively track the index by holding the same securities in the same proportions as the index. Index funds tend to have lower fees compared to actively managed funds and are a popular choice for investors seeking broad market exposure with minimal costs.

For example, an S&P 500 index fund will invest in the 500 largest U.S. companies included in the S&P 500 index, providing broad exposure to the U.S. stock market.

Sector Funds

Sector funds focus on a specific industry or sector of the economy, such as technology, healthcare, or energy. These funds allow investors to target investments in areas they believe will outperform the broader market. However, they also come with higher risk due to their concentrated exposure.

An investor bullish on the technology industry might choose a tech sector fund to capitalize on the growth potential of companies in this field.

International and Global Funds

International funds invest in companies located outside the investor's home country, while global funds invest in companies worldwide, including the home country. These funds provide diversification across different economies and markets, which can help reduce risk and enhance returns.

For example, a global fund might hold stocks from the U.S., Europe, and emerging markets, offering exposure to diverse economic conditions and growth opportunities.

Specialty Funds

Specialty funds invest in specific themes or strategies that don't fit neatly into other categories. These can include socially responsible funds, which invest based on environmental, social, and governance (ESG) criteria, or funds that focus on specific investment strategies like real estate or commodities.

An investor interested in ethical investing might choose a socially responsible fund that avoids companies with negative environmental or social impacts.

Each type of mutual fund offers different benefits and risks, catering to various investment goals and preferences. By understanding the characteristics of each type, you can better select the mutual funds that align with your financial objectives and risk tolerance.

How Mutual Funds Work

Mutual funds are investment vehicles that pool money from many investors to buy a diversified portfolio of securities. These funds are managed by professional fund managers who make decisions about which securities to buy and sell in order to achieve the fund's investment objectives. Mutual funds offer a simple and effective way for individuals to invest in a variety of assets without needing extensive knowledge or large amounts of capital.

The Basics of Mutual Funds

When you invest in a mutual fund, you are buying shares of the fund. Each share represents a portion of the fund's holdings. The value of these shares, known as the net asset value (NAV), changes daily based on the market value of the securities in the fund's portfolio. As the value of the underlying assets rises or falls, so does the NAV.

Types of Mutual Funds

There are several types of mutual funds, each with different investment strategies and objectives:

Equity Funds: These funds invest primarily in stocks. They can focus on specific sectors, such as technology or healthcare, or target specific market capitalizations, like small-cap or large-cap stocks.

Bond Funds: These funds invest in fixed-income securities, such as government bonds, corporate bonds, and municipal bonds. Bond funds aim to provide regular income and preserve capital.

Balanced Funds: Also known as hybrid funds, balanced funds invest in a mix of equities and bonds. They aim to provide a balance of income and capital appreciation while reducing risk through diversification.

Money Market Funds: These funds invest in short-term, high-quality debt instruments, such as Treasury bills and commercial paper. Money market funds are designed to provide liquidity and preserve capital while offering a modest return.

Index Funds: These funds aim to replicate the performance of a specific market index, such as the S&P 500. Index funds offer broad market exposure with lower management fees due to their passive management style.

Sector Funds: These funds focus on specific sectors of the economy, like energy, real estate, or technology. Sector funds can be more volatile due to their concentrated exposure.

How to Invest in Mutual Funds

Investing in mutual funds is straightforward. Here's how it typically works:

1. **Choosing a Fund**: Decide which type of mutual fund aligns with your investment goals, risk tolerance, and time horizon. Research different funds, looking at their past performance, fees, and the fund manager's track record.

2. **Opening an Account**: You can invest in mutual funds through various channels, including mutual fund companies, brokerage firms, and financial advisors. Open an account with your chosen provider if you don't already have one.

3. **Purchasing Shares**: Once your account is set up, you can buy shares of the mutual fund. You can invest a lump sum or set up automatic contributions to regularly invest a fixed amount.

4. **Monitoring Your Investment**: Regularly review your mutual fund investments to ensure they continue to align with your financial goals. Keep an eye on the fund's performance, fees, and any changes in the management team or investment strategy.

Benefits of Mutual Funds

Mutual funds offer several advantages for investors:

Diversification: By pooling money from many investors, mutual funds can invest in a wide variety of securities, reducing the risk associated with individual investments.

Professional Management: Experienced fund managers make investment decisions on behalf of investors, leveraging their expertise to manage the fund's portfolio effectively.

Accessibility: Mutual funds are accessible to individual investors with relatively small amounts of capital, allowing them to gain exposure to a diversified portfolio that would be difficult to achieve independently.

Liquidity: Mutual fund shares can typically be bought or sold on any business day, providing investors with liquidity and flexibility.

Convenience: Mutual funds simplify the investment process, handling the selection, buying, and selling of securities. This convenience makes them an attractive option for investors who prefer a hands-off approach.

Costs Associated with Mutual Funds

While mutual funds offer many benefits, it's important to be aware of the associated costs. These can include:

Management Fees: Annual fees paid to the fund manager for managing the fund. These are typically expressed as a percentage of the fund's assets and are known as the expense ratio.

Load Fees: Sales charges that may be applied when you buy (front-end load) or sell (back-end load) shares of the fund. No-load funds do not charge these fees.

12b-1 Fees: Marketing and distribution fees that are included in the fund's expense ratio.

Understanding these fees is crucial, as they can impact your overall returns. Always review a fund's prospectus for a detailed explanation of its fees and expenses.

Mutual funds provide a versatile and accessible investment option for building a diversified portfolio. By understanding how mutual funds work and the different types available, you can make informed decisions that align with your financial goals and risk tolerance.

Introduction to ETFs: What are ETFs?

Exchange-traded funds (ETFs) are investment funds that are traded on stock exchanges, much like individual stocks. ETFs hold a collection of assets such as stocks, bonds, or commodities and are designed to track the performance of a specific index, sector, or commodity. They offer a convenient way for investors to diversify their portfolios and gain exposure to various asset classes.

How ETFs Work

ETFs are created and managed by investment companies. These companies purchase a basket of assets that the ETF will track, and then issue shares that are traded on an exchange. Each share of an ETF represents a proportional ownership of the underlying assets. The price of an ETF share fluctuates throughout the trading day based on market demand and the value of the underlying assets.

For example, an ETF that tracks the S&P 500 will hold the same stocks in the same proportions as the S&P 500 index. If the S&P 500 rises or falls, the ETF's value will correspondingly rise or fall.

Benefits of ETFs

ETFs offer several advantages that make them attractive to investors:

1. **Diversification:** ETFs provide instant diversification by holding a wide range of assets within a single fund. This reduces the risk associated with investing in individual securities.

2. **Liquidity:** Because ETFs are traded on stock exchanges, they can be bought and sold throughout the trading day at market prices. This liquidity makes it easy for investors to enter and exit positions.

3. **Lower Costs:** ETFs generally have lower expense ratios compared to mutual funds because they are often passively managed. They also tend to have lower transaction costs.

4. **Transparency:** ETFs disclose their holdings daily, allowing investors to see exactly what assets are in the fund. This transparency helps investors make informed decisions.

5. **Flexibility:** Investors can use ETFs in various strategies, including long-term investing, short-term trading, hedging, and more. They can also be bought on margin and sold short, similar to individual stocks.

Types of ETFs

There are several types of ETFs, each designed to meet different investment needs and objectives:

- **Index ETFs:** These track a specific index, such as the S&P 500, Nasdaq-100, or Russell 2000. They aim to replicate the performance of the index by holding the same assets in the same proportions.

- **Sector and Industry ETFs:** These focus on specific sectors or industries, such as technology, healthcare, or energy. They allow investors to target areas they believe will outperform the broader market.

- **Bond ETFs:** These invest in bonds and other fixed-income securities. They can provide income and diversification within a bond portfolio.

- **Commodity ETFs:** These track the performance of commodities like gold, silver, oil, or agricultural products. They offer exposure to commodity markets without the need to physically own the commodities.

- **International ETFs:** These invest in assets outside the investor's home country. They provide exposure to global markets and can help diversify a portfolio.

- **Thematic ETFs:** These focus on specific investment themes or trends, such as clean energy, artificial intelligence, or cybersecurity. They allow investors to capitalize on emerging trends and innovations.

How to Invest in ETFs

Investing in ETFs is straightforward. You can purchase ETF shares through a brokerage account, just as you would with individual stocks. It's important to consider factors such as the ETF's expense ratio, tracking error (how well the ETF tracks its underlying index), and the liquidity of the ETF when making your decision.

For instance, if you want broad exposure to the U.S. stock market, you might choose an S&P 500 ETF. If you're interested in the technology sector, you could invest in a tech-focused ETF. Assessing your investment goals, risk tolerance, and market outlook will help you select the right ETFs for your portfolio.

ETFs offer a versatile and cost-effective way to build a diversified investment portfolio. By understanding what ETFs are and how they work, you can leverage their benefits to enhance your investment strategy and achieve your financial goals.

Differences Between ETFs and Mutual Funds

Exchange-traded funds (ETFs) and mutual funds are popular investment vehicles that offer investors access to a diversified portfolio of assets. While they share some similarities, there are key differences between the two that can impact your investment strategy and outcomes. Understanding these differences can help you choose the right option for your financial goals.

Structure and Trading

ETFs are traded on stock exchanges, similar to individual stocks. Investors can buy and sell ETF shares throughout the trading day at market prices, which can fluctuate based on supply and demand. This intraday trading provides flexibility and liquidity, allowing investors to react quickly to market changes.

Mutual funds, on the other hand, are not traded on exchanges. Investors buy and sell mutual fund shares directly from the fund company at the end of the trading day. The price at which mutual fund shares are bought or sold is determined by the fund's net asset value (NAV), which is calculated once daily after the market closes.

Management Style

Both ETFs and mutual funds can be either actively or passively managed. However, ETFs are more commonly associated with passive management. Passive ETFs aim to replicate the performance of a specific market index, such as the S&P 500, by holding a similar portfolio of assets. This approach typically results in lower management fees and expenses.

Mutual funds can also be passively managed (index funds) or actively managed. Actively managed mutual funds have fund managers who make investment decisions with the goal of outperforming the market. These funds often have higher fees due to the active management involved.

Fees and Expenses

The cost structure of ETFs and mutual funds can differ significantly. ETFs generally have lower expense ratios compared to mutual funds, particularly actively managed ones. This is because most ETFs are passively managed and have lower operational costs.

Mutual funds may charge various fees, including management fees, load fees (sales charges), and 12b-1 fees (marketing and distribution expenses). These fees can add up and impact your overall returns. It's important to review a fund's prospectus to understand the fees associated with it.

Minimum Investment Requirements

Mutual funds often have minimum investment requirements, which can range from a few hundred to several thousand dollars. This minimum investment can be a barrier for some investors, especially those just starting out.

ETFs, on the other hand, do not have minimum investment requirements beyond the cost of a single share, making them more accessible to a wider range of investors. This can be particularly advantageous for those looking to invest smaller amounts of money.

Tax Efficiency

ETFs are generally more tax-efficient than mutual funds. The structure of ETFs allows for in-kind creation and redemption processes, which can minimize the capital gains distributions that are passed on to investors. This means you may owe less in capital gains taxes when investing in ETFs.

Mutual funds, particularly actively managed ones, tend to have higher capital gains distributions because the fund manager is frequently buying and selling securities. These distributions are taxable events for investors, which can result in higher tax liabilities.

Dividend Reinvestment

Both ETFs and mutual funds offer dividend reinvestment options, but the process can differ. With mutual funds, dividends are typically reinvested automatically into additional shares of the fund at the NAV.

For ETFs, dividends can be reinvested through a dividend reinvestment plan (DRIP) offered by your brokerage. The timing and execution of dividend reinvestment can vary depending on the brokerage's policies, and not all brokerages offer DRIPs for all ETFs.

Transparency and Holdings Disclosure

ETFs generally provide greater transparency regarding their holdings. Most ETFs disclose their holdings daily, allowing investors to see exactly what assets the fund holds. This transparency can be beneficial for investors who want to closely monitor their investments.

Mutual funds typically disclose their holdings on a quarterly basis. While this is sufficient for many investors, those who prefer more frequent updates may find ETFs more appealing.

Flexibility and Use in Trading Strategies

ETFs offer greater flexibility for use in various trading strategies. Because they are traded like stocks, investors can employ techniques such as short selling, margin trading, and using stop-loss orders with ETFs. This flexibility makes ETFs suitable for both long-term investors and those who engage in more active trading.

Mutual funds are generally designed for long-term investment and do not offer the same flexibility for active trading strategies. They are better suited for investors who prefer a buy-and-hold approach.

ETFs and mutual funds each have their own unique characteristics and advantages. Understanding the differences between them can help you make informed decisions and select the investment vehicle that best aligns with your financial goals and investment style. Whether you prioritize lower costs, tax efficiency, or trading flexibility, knowing these key distinctions will guide you in building a successful investment portfolio.

Selecting Funds for Your Portfolio: Active vs. Passive Management

When it comes to managing mutual funds and ETFs, there are two primary approaches: active management and passive management. Each approach has its own philosophy, advantages, and drawbacks, and understanding the differences can help you choose the right funds for your investment goals.

Active Management

Active management involves a team of professional portfolio managers making investment decisions with the goal of outperforming a specific benchmark index. These managers conduct thorough research, analyze market trends, and use their expertise to select securities they believe will provide the best returns.

Active managers strive to capitalize on market inefficiencies and identify undervalued or overvalued securities. They adjust the fund's holdings frequently based on market conditions and their predictions about future performance.

For example, an actively managed equity fund might have a manager who selects stocks they believe are poised for growth based on in-depth company analysis and market forecasts. The manager might increase the fund's allocation to technology stocks if they believe that sector will outperform in the coming years.

Advantages of Active Management

1. **Potential for Outperformance:** Skilled managers can potentially achieve higher returns than the market average by making informed investment decisions and exploiting market inefficiencies.

2. **Flexibility:** Active managers can quickly respond to changing market conditions and adjust the fund's holdings to mitigate risk or seize opportunities.

3. **Expertise:** Investors benefit from the professional knowledge and experience of the fund managers, who dedicate significant time and resources to research and analysis.

Drawbacks of Active Management

1. **Higher Costs:** Active management usually comes with higher fees due to the extensive research and trading involved. These fees can eat into overall returns.

2. **Risk of Underperformance:** Even skilled managers can make mistakes, and not all actively managed funds outperform their benchmarks. Poor investment choices can lead to underperformance.

3. **Inconsistent Returns:** Performance can vary significantly from year to year, making it harder to predict long-term outcomes.

Passive Management

Passive management, also known as index investing, aims to replicate the performance of a specific benchmark index, such as the S&P 500 or the Nasdaq-100. Instead of trying to beat the market, passive managers focus on matching the index's returns by holding the same securities in the same proportions as the index.

Passive funds, such as index funds and ETFs, have a buy-and-hold strategy, meaning they make fewer trades and typically have lower operating costs. These funds are designed to provide broad market exposure and are ideal for investors seeking steady, long-term growth.

For instance, a passive S&P 500 index fund will invest in all 500 companies within the S&P 500 index, providing diversification across large-cap U.S. stocks.

Advantages of Passive Management

1. **Lower Costs:** Passive funds generally have lower expense ratios because they require less research and trading. Lower costs mean more of your investment returns stay in your pocket.

2. **Consistent Performance:** Passive funds aim to match the performance of their benchmark index, providing predictable returns that reflect the overall market's performance.

3. **Simplicity:** With a straightforward investment strategy, passive funds are easy to understand and manage.

Drawbacks of Passive Management

1. **Limited Flexibility:** Passive funds are bound to their index and cannot adjust holdings based on market conditions or economic forecasts. This means they cannot capitalize on short-term opportunities or avoid potential losses in declining sectors.

2. **Average Returns:** By design, passive funds aim to match the market's performance, not exceed it. Investors

seeking to outperform the market might find passive funds limiting.

Choosing Between Active and Passive Management

The choice between active and passive management depends on your investment goals, risk tolerance, and personal preferences. Some investors prefer the potential for higher returns and the professional expertise offered by active management, despite the higher costs and risks. Others favor the lower costs, simplicity, and consistent performance of passive management.

Many investors opt for a combination of both strategies, diversifying their portfolios with a mix of actively managed funds and passive index funds. This approach can balance the potential for outperformance with the stability and cost-efficiency of passive investing.

Active and passive management each offer unique benefits and challenges. Understanding these differences can help you make informed decisions and select the right mix of funds to achieve your financial objectives.

Evaluating Fund Performance

Evaluating the performance of mutual funds and ETFs is essential for making informed investment decisions. A thorough evaluation helps you determine whether a fund aligns with your financial goals, risk tolerance, and investment strategy. Here are some key factors to consider when assessing fund performance.

Historical Performance

Analyzing a fund's historical performance is a good starting point. Look at the fund's returns over various periods, such as one year, three years, five years, and since inception. While past performance is not a guarantee of future results, it provides insight into how the fund has performed in different market conditions. Compare the fund's performance to its benchmark index and peer group to see how it stacks up against similar investments.

Risk-Adjusted Returns

It's important to consider not just the returns, but also the level of risk taken to achieve those returns. Risk-adjusted return metrics help you understand how well a fund compensates investors for the risk taken. Common risk-adjusted measures include:

Sharpe Ratio: This ratio measures the fund's return relative to its risk, as indicated by its standard deviation. A higher Sharpe ratio indicates better risk-adjusted performance.

Alpha: Alpha represents the fund's performance relative to its benchmark, adjusted for risk. Positive alpha indicates the fund has outperformed its benchmark, while negative alpha indicates underperformance.

Beta: Beta measures the fund's sensitivity to market movements. A beta of 1 indicates the fund moves with the market, while a beta greater than 1 suggests higher volatility. Funds with lower beta values tend to be less volatile.

Expense Ratios

The expense ratio represents the annual cost of owning the fund, expressed as a percentage of the fund's assets. Lower expense ratios are generally more favorable, as high costs can erode returns over time. Compare the fund's expense ratio to similar funds to ensure it is competitive. Keep in mind that actively managed funds typically have higher expense ratios than passively managed funds or ETFs.

Management Team

The expertise and stability of the fund's management team play a crucial role in its performance. Look for information about the fund manager's experience, track record, and tenure with the fund. Consistency in management can be a positive indicator, as it suggests a stable investment strategy. Frequent changes in management might indicate potential disruptions or shifts in strategy.

Portfolio Composition

Review the fund's portfolio composition to understand its investment strategy and diversification. Analyze the types of securities held, sector allocations, and geographic exposure. A well-diversified portfolio can help mitigate risk. Pay attention to any significant concentrations in specific sectors or regions, as these can increase the fund's volatility.

Turnover Ratio

The turnover ratio measures how frequently the fund buys and sells securities within a year. A high turnover ratio can indicate active trading, which may lead to higher transaction costs and capital gains distributions. These costs can impact the fund's overall returns. Low turnover ratios generally suggest a more stable, long-term investment approach.

Income Distribution

Evaluate the fund's income distribution history, especially if you are looking for regular income from your investments. Check the frequency and amount of dividends or interest payments. Funds that consistently distribute income can be attractive for income-focused investors.

Performance Consistency

Assess the fund's consistency by examining its performance across different market cycles. Look for funds that have demonstrated the ability to perform well in both bull and bear markets. Consistent performance can indicate a robust investment strategy that adapts well to changing market conditions.

Peer Comparison

Comparing the fund to its peers provides context for its performance. Use performance metrics to see how the fund ranks within its category. Peer comparison helps you identify whether the fund is a top performer or lagging behind similar funds. Tools like Morningstar or Lipper ratings can be useful for this purpose.

Evaluating fund performance requires a comprehensive approach, considering both quantitative and qualitative factors. By examining historical performance, risk-adjusted returns, expense ratios, management expertise, portfolio composition, and other key metrics, you can make more informed decisions and select funds that align with your investment goals. This thorough evaluation process helps ensure that your investments are well-positioned to achieve long-term success.

Chapter 6: Real Estate and Alternative Investments

Investing in Real Estate: Residential vs. Commercial Real Estate

Investing in real estate can be a lucrative way to build wealth and generate income. Real estate investments typically fall into two main categories: residential and commercial. Each type has its own characteristics, benefits, and challenges, making it important to understand the differences before deciding where to invest.

Residential Real Estate

Residential real estate includes properties designed for people to live in. This category encompasses single-family homes, multi-family homes (like duplexes and triplexes), townhouses, condominiums, and apartments.

Characteristics of Residential Real Estate

1. **Tenant Type:** Residential properties are leased to individuals or families. The demand for housing is generally stable, as everyone needs a place to live.

2. **Lease Terms:** Leases for residential properties are usually shorter, often ranging from one year to month-to-month agreements. This can lead to more frequent tenant turnover.

3. **Financing:** Mortgages for residential properties are typically easier to obtain than commercial loans. There are also more financing options, including FHA and VA loans for qualified buyers.

4. **Maintenance and Management:** Managing residential properties can be more hands-on, requiring regular maintenance, tenant interactions, and handling day-to-day issues.

Benefits of Residential Real Estate

1. **Stable Demand:** The constant need for housing ensures a relatively steady demand for residential properties.

2. **Financing Availability:** Easier access to financing options makes it more accessible for individual investors.

3. **Tenant Variety:** With a large pool of potential tenants, it's often easier to find renters for residential properties.

Challenges of Residential Real Estate

1. **High Tenant Turnover:** Shorter lease terms can result in more frequent vacancies and the need to find new tenants regularly.

2. **Management Intensive:** Managing residential properties can be time-consuming, especially with multiple units or frequent tenant issues.

3. **Market Fluctuations:** The value of residential properties can be influenced by local market conditions, such as employment rates and local economic health.

Commercial Real Estate

Commercial real estate includes properties used for business purposes. This category covers office buildings, retail spaces, warehouses, industrial properties, and multi-family properties with more than four units.

Characteristics of Commercial Real Estate

1. **Tenant Type:** Commercial properties are leased to businesses, which can range from small startups to large corporations.

2. **Lease Terms:** Commercial leases tend to be longer, often ranging from five to ten years or more. This provides more stability and predictability in rental income.

3. **Financing:** Obtaining financing for commercial properties can be more complex and often requires larger down payments and higher interest rates. Lenders typically look at the property's income potential and the financial stability of the tenants.

4. **Maintenance and Management:** Managing commercial properties can be less hands-on compared to residential, as many leases require tenants to handle maintenance and repairs.

Benefits of Commercial Real Estate

1. **Longer Leases:** Longer lease terms provide more stable and predictable cash flow.

2. **Higher Income Potential:** Commercial properties often generate higher rental income compared to residential properties.

3. **Professional Tenants:** Businesses tend to be more reliable tenants, and commercial leases often include clauses that make tenants responsible for property upkeep.

Challenges of Commercial Real Estate

1. **Higher Risk:** Economic downturns can lead to higher vacancy rates and decreased rental income in commercial properties.

2. **Complex Financing:** Securing loans for commercial properties can be more challenging and require more extensive financial scrutiny.

3. **Market Sensitivity:** Commercial real estate is highly sensitive to economic cycles, and vacancies can be longer during economic downturns.

Choosing Between Residential and Commercial Real Estate

The choice between residential and commercial real estate depends on your investment goals, risk tolerance, and management preferences. Residential real estate might be more suitable for those seeking steady demand and easier financing, while commercial real estate can offer higher income potential and longer lease stability but comes with higher risks and complexities.

Investing in real estate, whether residential or commercial, can diversify your portfolio and provide opportunities for income and appreciation. By understanding the unique aspects of each type, you can make more informed decisions and tailor your investment strategy to meet your financial objectives.

REITs: Real Estate Investment Trusts

Real Estate Investment Trusts (REITs) offer investors a way to invest in real estate without the need to purchase and manage properties directly. REITs own, operate, or finance income-producing real estate across various sectors, such as residential, commercial, industrial, and retail properties. Investing in REITs can provide both diversification and income, making them an attractive option for many investors.

What Are REITs?

REITs are companies that own, manage, or finance real estate properties. They operate similarly to mutual funds, pooling capital from numerous investors to purchase a diversified portfolio of properties. REITs generate income primarily through renting, leasing, or selling the properties they own, and they are required by law to distribute at least 90% of their taxable income to shareholders as dividends.

Types of REITs

There are several types of REITs, each focusing on different aspects of the real estate market:

Equity REITs: These REITs own and operate income-producing real estate. They generate revenue through rent collected from tenants. Equity REITs can invest in various property types, including residential apartments, office buildings, shopping malls, and hotels.

Mortgage REITs (mREITs): Instead of owning properties, mortgage REITs provide financing for income-producing real estate by purchasing or originating mortgages and mortgage-backed securities. They earn income from the interest on these loans.

Hybrid REITs: These REITs combine the characteristics of both equity and mortgage REITs. They invest in properties and hold mortgages, offering a diversified approach to real estate investment.

Benefits of Investing in REITs

Investing in REITs offers several advantages:

Diversification: REITs provide exposure to the real estate market, which can diversify your investment portfolio beyond traditional stocks and bonds. This diversification can help reduce risk and improve overall portfolio performance.

Regular Income: REITs are known for their high dividend yields. Since they are required to distribute a significant portion of their income to shareholders, REITs can provide a steady stream of income, making them attractive to income-focused investors.

Liquidity: Unlike direct real estate investments, which can be illiquid and time-consuming to sell, REITs are traded on major stock exchanges. This liquidity allows investors to buy and sell shares easily, providing flexibility and quick access to capital.

Professional Management: REITs are managed by experienced professionals who handle property acquisition, leasing, maintenance, and financing. This professional management can lead to better performance and reduced hassle for individual investors.

Risks of Investing in REITs

While REITs offer many benefits, they also come with risks:

Market Risk: REIT prices can be volatile, influenced by changes in the real estate market, interest rates, and the broader economy. Economic downturns or declines in property values can negatively impact REIT performance.

Interest Rate Risk: REITs are sensitive to interest rate changes. Rising interest rates can increase borrowing costs for REITs and make their dividend yields less attractive compared to other fixed-income investments, potentially leading to lower share prices.

Sector-Specific Risk: Some REITs focus on specific sectors, such as retail or office spaces. Changes in market conditions or consumer behavior affecting these sectors can impact the performance of sector-specific REITs.

How to Invest in REITs

Investing in REITs is straightforward and can be done through several methods:

Direct Purchase: You can buy shares of publicly traded REITs on stock exchanges through a brokerage account. This method provides flexibility in choosing specific REITs that align with your investment goals.

REIT Mutual Funds: These funds pool money from multiple investors to invest in a diversified portfolio of REITs. REIT mutual funds offer diversification and professional management, making them suitable for investors seeking broad exposure to the real estate market.

REIT ETFs: Exchange-traded funds (ETFs) that focus on REITs provide similar benefits to REIT mutual funds but with the added flexibility of intraday trading. REIT ETFs often have lower fees and can be a cost-effective way to invest in a diversified portfolio of REITs.

Evaluating REITs

When selecting REITs, consider factors such as the quality and location of the properties, the experience of the management team, and the REIT's historical performance. Assess the dividend yield and payout ratio to understand the income potential and sustainability. Additionally, examine the REIT's debt levels and financial health to gauge its ability to withstand economic downturns.

REITs offer a convenient and effective way to invest in real estate, providing diversification, income, and liquidity. By understanding the types of REITs available and carefully evaluating their performance and risks, you can incorporate REITs into your investment portfolio to achieve your financial objectives.

Commodities and Other Alternatives: Gold, Silver, and Other Commodities

Investing in commodities like gold, silver, and other physical assets offers a way to diversify your portfolio and hedge against inflation and economic uncertainty. These tangible assets have intrinsic value and can provide stability during market volatility.

Gold

Gold has been a valuable asset for thousands of years, serving as a store of value, a medium of exchange, and a symbol of wealth. Today, gold remains a popular investment for several reasons:

1. **Hedge Against Inflation:** Gold often retains its value over time, making it a good hedge against inflation. When the value of fiat currencies declines, the price of gold typically rises.

2. **Safe Haven:** During economic uncertainty or geopolitical instability, investors flock to gold as a safe-haven asset. This demand can drive up gold prices during market downturns.

3. **Liquidity:** Gold is highly liquid, meaning it can be easily bought and sold in global markets.

Investing in gold can be done in various ways, including buying physical gold (coins, bars, jewelry), investing in gold ETFs (exchange-traded funds), or purchasing shares in gold mining companies.

Silver

Silver is another precious metal with significant industrial applications, making it unique compared to gold. Silver is used in electronics, solar panels, medical devices, and various other industries. This dual role as both an investment and an industrial commodity influences its price movements.

1. **Industrial Demand:** Silver's extensive use in industrial applications can drive demand and impact prices. Economic growth and technological advancements often lead to increased silver consumption.

2. **Affordability:** Silver is generally more affordable than gold, allowing investors to buy larger quantities with less capital.

3. **Hedge and Safe Haven:** Like gold, silver also serves as a hedge against inflation and a safe-haven asset during times of economic uncertainty.

Investors can buy physical silver, invest in silver ETFs, or purchase shares in silver mining companies to gain exposure to this metal.

Other Commodities

Beyond gold and silver, there are numerous other commodities that investors can consider. These include energy commodities like oil and natural gas, agricultural commodities like wheat and corn, and industrial metals like copper and platinum.

1. **Oil:** Oil is a critical energy commodity with prices influenced by global supply and demand, geopolitical events, and economic conditions. Investing in oil can be done through futures contracts, ETFs, or shares in oil companies.

2. **Natural Gas:** Natural gas is another important energy source, with prices affected by factors such as weather,

production levels, and regulatory changes. Investors can access natural gas through futures, ETFs, or stocks in natural gas companies.

3. **Agricultural Commodities:** Wheat, corn, soybeans, and other agricultural products are essential for global food supply. Prices are driven by weather conditions, crop yields, and global demand. Investments can be made through futures contracts, ETFs, or stocks in agribusiness companies.

4. **Industrial Metals:** Metals like copper, platinum, and palladium are used in various industrial applications. Their prices are influenced by industrial demand, mining output, and technological advancements. Investors can buy these metals through futures, ETFs, or shares in mining companies.

Benefits of Commodity Investing

Investing in commodities can offer several advantages:

1. **Diversification:** Commodities often have low correlation with traditional asset classes like stocks and bonds, providing diversification benefits.

2. **Inflation Protection:** Commodities tend to perform well during periods of high inflation, as their prices often rise when the cost of goods and services increases.

3. **Potential for High Returns:** Commodities can experience significant price swings, offering opportunities for substantial gains.

Risks of Commodity Investing

However, commodity investing also comes with risks:

1. **Volatility:** Commodity prices can be highly volatile, influenced by a wide range of factors including geopolitical events, weather conditions, and changes in supply and demand.

2. **Market Complexity:** Understanding the commodity markets requires knowledge of various factors that impact prices, making it more complex than traditional stock or bond investing.

3. **Storage and Transportation:** Physical commodities like gold, silver, and oil require storage and transportation, adding additional costs and logistical challenges.

Investing in commodities like gold, silver, and other physical assets can be a valuable part of a diversified portfolio. They offer unique benefits, including protection against inflation and economic uncertainty, but also come with their own set of risks and complexities. By carefully considering these factors, you can determine the best way to incorporate commodities into your investment strategy.

Cryptocurrencies and Digital Assets

Cryptocurrencies and digital assets have emerged as a new and dynamic class of investments over the past decade. These assets are based on blockchain technology, which provides a decentralized and secure method for recording transactions. The most well-known cryptocurrency is Bitcoin, but there are thousands of others, including Ethereum, Ripple (XRP), and Litecoin.

What are Cryptocurrencies?

Cryptocurrencies are digital or virtual currencies that use cryptography for security. Unlike traditional currencies issued by governments, cryptocurrencies operate on decentralized networks using blockchain technology. This decentralization makes them resistant to censorship and fraud.

Blockchain Technology

Blockchain is a distributed ledger technology that records transactions across multiple computers. Each block contains a list of transactions, and once a block is completed, it is added to the chain of previous blocks. This structure ensures transparency and security, as altering any information on the blockchain would require altering all subsequent blocks, which is practically impossible.

For instance, Bitcoin transactions are verified by network nodes through cryptography and recorded in a public distributed ledger called a blockchain. This process ensures the integrity and chronological order of transactions, making Bitcoin highly secure.

Popular Cryptocurrencies

1. **Bitcoin (BTC):** Bitcoin was the first cryptocurrency, created in 2009 by an anonymous person or group known as Satoshi Nakamoto. It is often referred to as digital gold due to its limited supply and store of value properties.

2. **Ethereum (ETH):** Ethereum is a decentralized platform that enables smart contracts and decentralized

applications (DApps) to be built and run without any downtime, fraud, or interference. Its native cryptocurrency, Ether, is used to power the platform.

3. **Ripple (XRP):** Ripple is both a platform and a currency. The Ripple platform is an open-source protocol designed for fast and cheap digital transactions, primarily for cross-border payments.

4. **Litecoin (LTC):** Created by Charlie Lee in 2011, Litecoin is a peer-to-peer cryptocurrency that allows instant, near-zero cost payments to anyone in the world. It is an early spinoff of Bitcoin, often considered the silver to Bitcoin's gold.

Benefits of Investing in Cryptocurrencies

1. **High Return Potential:** Cryptocurrencies have shown the potential for high returns. Bitcoin, for example, has appreciated significantly since its inception, making early investors substantial profits.

2. **Decentralization:** Being decentralized means cryptocurrencies are not controlled by any single entity, reducing the risk of government interference or manipulation.

3. **Liquidity:** Many cryptocurrencies can be easily bought and sold on various exchanges, providing liquidity to investors.

Risks of Investing in Cryptocurrencies

1. **Volatility:** Cryptocurrencies are highly volatile, with prices capable of swinging dramatically in short periods. This volatility can result in significant gains but also substantial losses.

2. **Regulatory Risks:** The regulatory environment for cryptocurrencies is still evolving. Future regulations could impact their value and accessibility.

3. **Security Risks:** While blockchain technology is secure, the exchanges and wallets used to store cryptocurrencies can be vulnerable to hacks and thefts.

Digital Assets Beyond Cryptocurrencies

Digital assets encompass more than just cryptocurrencies. They include tokens, digital securities, and digital collectibles (NFTs).

1. **Tokens:** Tokens are digital assets created on existing blockchains, such as Ethereum. They can represent

various assets or utilities, such as access to a specific service or voting rights in a decentralized organization.

2. **Digital Securities:** Also known as security tokens, these represent traditional financial assets like stocks or bonds but are issued and traded on a blockchain. They combine the benefits of blockchain technology with the regulatory assurances of traditional securities.

3. **Non-Fungible Tokens (NFTs):** NFTs are unique digital assets that represent ownership of a specific item or piece of content, such as art, music, or virtual real estate. Unlike cryptocurrencies, NFTs are indivisible and unique, making them ideal for representing rare items.

How to Invest in Cryptocurrencies and Digital Assets

Investing in cryptocurrencies and digital assets can be done through various platforms and methods:

1. **Cryptocurrency Exchanges:** Platforms like Coinbase, Binance, and Kraken allow you to buy, sell, and trade a wide range of cryptocurrencies.

2. **Wallets:** Secure wallets, both hardware and software-based, are essential for storing your digital assets safely.

Hardware wallets like Ledger and Trezor offer high security.

3. **Initial Coin Offerings (ICOs) and Token Sales:** These are fundraising methods for new cryptocurrency projects. Investors can purchase tokens at an early stage, potentially at a lower price.

Cryptocurrencies and digital assets offer a new frontier for investors, combining high potential returns with significant risks. Understanding the underlying technology, the market dynamics, and the specific characteristics of each digital asset is crucial for making informed investment decisions. As the digital asset space continues to evolve, it offers exciting opportunities for those willing to navigate its complexities.

Benefits and Risks of Alternative Investments: Diversification Benefits

Diversification is a fundamental investment strategy that involves spreading your investments across different asset classes, sectors, and geographic regions. The primary goal is to reduce risk by ensuring that the performance of one investment does not heavily impact your overall portfolio. Diversification can enhance returns while mitigating the volatility that comes with investing in a single asset or market.

Risk Reduction

One of the key benefits of diversification is risk reduction. By investing in a variety of assets, you minimize the impact of a poor performance in any one investment. For example, if your portfolio includes stocks, bonds, real estate, and commodities, a downturn in the stock market may be offset by stable or rising values in the other asset classes.

Smoother Returns

Diversification tends to smooth out the returns of your portfolio. Different assets perform differently under various economic conditions. Stocks might perform well during economic expansions, while bonds could provide stability during downturns. Real estate and commodities often have their own cycles, independent of traditional markets. By holding a mix of these assets, your overall portfolio is likely to experience less dramatic fluctuations in value.

Exposure to Growth Opportunities

Diversification also allows you to tap into growth opportunities across various sectors and regions. While some markets may be experiencing slow growth or stagnation, others might be booming. For instance, investing in international stocks can give you exposure to fast-growing economies that you might miss if you only invest domestically. This broader exposure increases the potential for higher returns.

Preservation of Capital

By spreading investments across different asset classes, diversification helps preserve capital during volatile market periods. If one sector or asset class suffers significant losses, the more stable performance of other investments can help cushion the blow. This preservation is particularly important for long-term investors who need to protect their capital to meet future financial goals.

Enhanced Risk-Adjusted Returns

Diversification can improve the risk-adjusted returns of your portfolio. This means that for a given level of risk, a diversified portfolio can achieve higher returns than a non-diversified one. By combining assets that react differently to various market conditions, you can enhance your portfolio's performance without taking on additional risk.

Practical Example of Diversification

Consider an investor with a diversified portfolio that includes:

- **Stocks:** Provides potential for high returns through capital appreciation.

- **Bonds:** Offers steady income and helps stabilize the portfolio during market volatility.

- **Real Estate:** Adds tangible assets that can appreciate over time and generate rental income.

- **Commodities:** Acts as a hedge against inflation and economic uncertainty.

In this diversified portfolio, if the stock market experiences a downturn, the bonds might maintain their value or even increase, providing a counterbalance. Real estate and commodities could also perform differently, depending on economic conditions, further stabilizing the overall portfolio.

Strategic Asset Allocation

Effective diversification involves strategic asset allocation, where you decide the percentage of your portfolio to invest in each asset class based on your risk tolerance, investment goals, and time horizon. Regularly reviewing and rebalancing your portfolio ensures that your asset allocation remains aligned with your objectives.

For example, a young investor with a high risk tolerance and a long time horizon might allocate more to stocks and real estate, aiming for higher growth. An investor nearing retirement might shift more into bonds and dividend-paying stocks to prioritize income and capital preservation.

Mitigating Systematic and Unsystematic Risk

Diversification helps mitigate both systematic and unsystematic risk. Systematic risk, or market risk, affects all investments in the market and cannot be eliminated. However, unsystematic risk, or specific risk, is tied to individual investments and can be reduced through diversification. By holding a variety of investments, you lower the impact of any one investment's poor performance on your overall portfolio.

Diversification is a powerful strategy to manage risk, stabilize returns, and capture growth opportunities. By thoughtfully spreading your investments across different asset classes and regularly reviewing your portfolio, you can achieve a balanced and resilient investment strategy.

Understanding the Risks

Investing in alternative assets like real estate, commodities, and cryptocurrencies can offer substantial rewards, but it also comes with a unique set of risks. It's essential to understand these risks to make informed decisions and protect your investments.

Market Volatility

Alternative investments often experience higher volatility compared to traditional assets like stocks and bonds. Prices can fluctuate widely due to various factors such as economic changes, geopolitical events, or market sentiment. For example, cryptocurrency prices can swing dramatically within a single day, influenced by news, regulatory developments, or changes in investor sentiment.

Liquidity Risks

Many alternative investments are less liquid than traditional securities. This means they can be harder to buy or sell quickly without affecting their price. Real estate, for instance, requires time to sell, which can be a disadvantage if you need quick access to cash. Similarly, some collectibles or private equity investments may have limited buyers, making it difficult to sell at your desired price.

Regulatory Risks

Regulatory environments for alternative investments can be uncertain and rapidly changing. Cryptocurrencies face significant regulatory scrutiny worldwide, and new laws can impact their value and how they can be traded. Real estate investments are subject to local property laws and taxes, which can change and affect your investment returns. Keeping abreast of regulatory changes is crucial for managing these risks.

Economic and Market Risks

Economic downturns can significantly affect the value of alternative investments. Real estate markets can suffer during recessions, leading to decreased property values and rental incomes. Commodities like oil and agricultural products are sensitive to global economic conditions and supply-demand dynamics. A slowdown in the economy can reduce demand for these commodities, impacting their prices.

Operational Risks

Managing alternative investments often requires specialized knowledge and expertise. Real estate investments require property management skills, dealing with tenants, maintenance, and local regulations. Commodities trading involves understanding market trends and supply chains. Lacking the necessary expertise can lead to poor investment decisions and financial losses.

Fraud and Security Risks

Alternative investments, particularly digital assets like cryptocurrencies, can be susceptible to fraud and hacking. Cryptocurrency exchanges and wallets can be targets for cyber-attacks, potentially leading to significant losses. Conducting thorough due diligence and using secure, reputable platforms are essential to mitigate these risks.

Diversification Challenges

While alternative investments can diversify your portfolio, they can also pose challenges in achieving balanced diversification. The correlation between alternative assets and traditional securities can change, especially during market stress, potentially reducing the effectiveness of diversification. Ensuring a well-diversified portfolio requires careful planning and regular review.

Valuation Difficulties

Determining the value of alternative investments can be more complex than valuing stocks or bonds. Real estate values depend on local market conditions, property conditions, and other factors. Commodities prices fluctuate based on global supply and demand, while the value of collectibles or art can be highly subjective. Accurate valuation is crucial for making informed investment decisions.

Tax Implications

Alternative investments often have different tax implications compared to traditional investments. Real estate investments can come with property taxes, capital gains taxes, and potential depreciation benefits. Cryptocurrencies are subject to capital gains taxes, and tax laws can vary widely by jurisdiction.

Understanding the tax treatment of your investments is important for maximizing after-tax returns.

Investment Horizon

Many alternative investments require a long-term commitment to realize their full potential. Real estate projects, for instance, may take years to appreciate in value or generate substantial rental income. Patience and a long-term perspective are essential when investing in these assets.

Understanding the risks associated with alternative investments helps you make informed decisions and develop strategies to mitigate these risks. Thorough research, diversification, and professional advice can enhance your ability to navigate the complexities of alternative investments and achieve your financial goals.

Chapter 7: Advanced Strategies and Tools

Leveraging Technology in Investing: Robo-Advisors

Robo-advisors are digital platforms that provide automated, algorithm-driven financial planning services with little to no human supervision. These platforms use advanced algorithms to build and manage a diversified investment portfolio based on your financial goals, risk tolerance, and time horizon.

How Robo-Advisors Work

Robo-advisors start by gathering information from you through an online survey. This survey typically includes questions about your financial goals, investment time frame, risk tolerance, and other personal financial information. Based on your responses, the robo-advisor creates a personalized investment plan. The platform then automatically invests your money in a diversified portfolio of low-cost exchange-traded funds (ETFs) or index funds, aligning with your risk profile and objectives.

For example, if you indicate a high risk tolerance and a long investment horizon, the robo-advisor might allocate a larger portion of your portfolio to equities. Conversely, if you have a low risk tolerance or a shorter time frame, the portfolio might be more heavily weighted towards bonds and other fixed-income assets.

Advantages of Robo-Advisors

1. **Low Fees:** One of the most significant benefits of robo-advisors is their cost-effectiveness. Traditional financial advisors can charge high management fees, typically around 1% of your assets under management. Robo-advisors, on the other hand, often charge significantly lower fees, sometimes as low as 0.25% to 0.50%.

2. **Accessibility:** Robo-advisors make investing accessible to a broader audience. Many platforms have low or no minimum investment requirements, allowing individuals with modest amounts of capital to start investing.

3. **Ease of Use:** These platforms are user-friendly and convenient, making it easy for anyone to set up and manage an investment portfolio. The entire process, from signing up to monitoring your investments, can be done online.

4. **Automatic Rebalancing:** Robo-advisors automatically rebalance your portfolio to maintain your desired asset allocation. This means they periodically adjust the proportions of different assets in your portfolio to align with your investment goals and risk tolerance, without you having to lift a finger.

5. **Tax-Loss Harvesting:** Many robo-advisors offer tax-loss harvesting, a strategy that involves selling securities at a loss to offset capital gains taxes. This can help improve your after-tax returns.

Considerations When Using Robo-Advisors

1. **Limited Personalization:** While robo-advisors provide a high level of automation and convenience, they might lack the personalized advice that a human financial advisor can offer. If you have complex financial needs or prefer a more tailored approach, a traditional advisor might be better suited for you.

2. **Market Limitations:** Robo-advisors typically invest in ETFs and index funds, which means you might miss out on the potential gains from individual stocks or other investment opportunities that require active management.

3. **Algorithm Reliance:** Robo-advisors rely on algorithms and historical data to make investment decisions. While these tools are sophisticated, they may not always account for sudden market changes or unique personal circumstances.

Choosing a Robo-Advisor

When selecting a robo-advisor, consider the following factors:

- **Fees:** Compare the management fees and additional costs associated with different platforms.

- **Features:** Look for features that match your needs, such as tax-loss harvesting, automatic rebalancing, and access to human advisors for additional guidance.

- **Performance:** Review the historical performance of the robo-advisor, keeping in mind that past performance is not indicative of future results.

- **User Experience:** Choose a platform that you find easy to navigate and use.

For example, popular robo-advisors like Betterment, Wealthfront, and Vanguard Personal Advisor Services each offer unique features and fee structures. Betterment is known for its user-friendly interface and comprehensive financial planning tools, while Wealthfront excels in tax optimization features. Vanguard offers a hybrid service, combining automated investing with access to human financial advisors.

Robo-advisors provide a convenient and cost-effective way to manage your investments. By leveraging technology, these platforms democratize access to professional investment management, making it easier for individuals to achieve their financial goals. Whether you're a novice investor looking for an easy entry point or an experienced investor seeking low-cost portfolio management, robo-advisors can be a valuable tool in your investment arsenal.

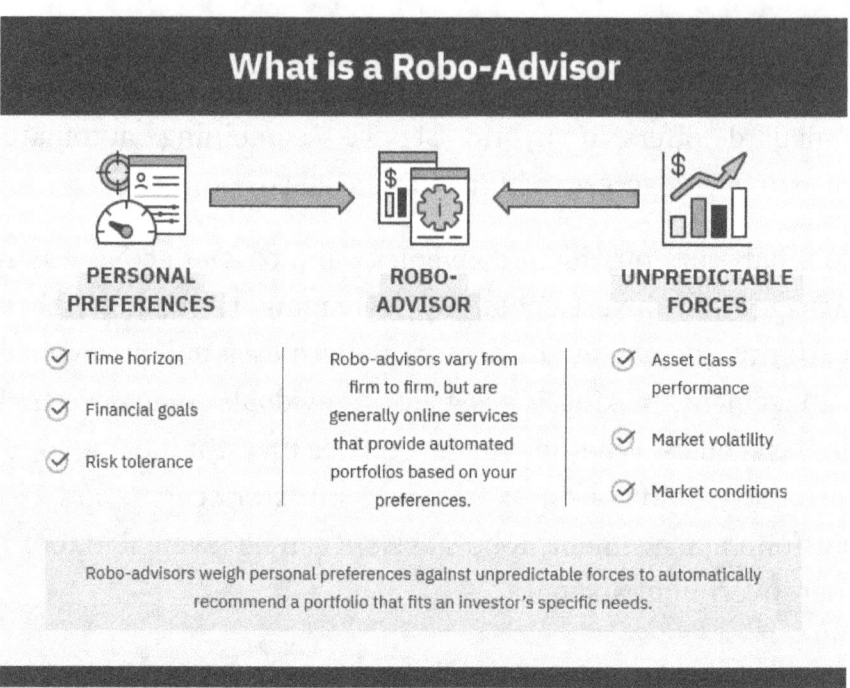

How Do Robo-Advisors Work. Source: tokenist.com

Using Investment Apps

Investment apps have revolutionized the way people manage their finances and invest in the markets. These apps offer a range of features designed to simplify investing, making it accessible to both beginners and experienced investors. Here's how you can effectively use investment apps to enhance your investment strategy.

Accessibility and Convenience

Investment apps provide the convenience of managing your investments from your smartphone or tablet. This allows you to monitor your portfolio, execute trades, and stay updated with market news anytime and anywhere. The ease of access means you can quickly respond to market changes and make informed decisions without needing a computer.

Real-Time Data and Alerts

Most investment apps offer real-time data on stock prices, market trends, and financial news. This immediate access to information helps you stay informed about market movements and company performance. Additionally, you can set up custom alerts for specific stocks or market conditions. These alerts notify you of significant price changes, earnings reports, or other relevant events, enabling timely actions.

Research and Analysis Tools

Many investment apps include built-in research and analysis tools. These tools provide access to financial statements, analyst ratings, historical performance data, and technical analysis charts. Utilizing these resources can help you make better investment decisions by providing a comprehensive understanding of the assets you are considering.

For example, if you are interested in a particular stock, the app can provide its historical performance, earnings reports, and analyst recommendations, helping you decide whether it aligns with your investment goals.

Automated Investing

Some investment apps offer automated investing services, often referred to as robo-advisors. These services use algorithms to create and manage a diversified portfolio based on your risk tolerance, financial goals, and investment horizon. Robo-advisors can be an excellent option for investors who prefer a hands-off approach, as they handle asset allocation, rebalancing, and tax optimization.

By answering a few questions about your financial situation and goals, a robo-advisor can design a personalized investment plan and automatically adjust your portfolio as needed.

Fractional Shares

Investment apps often allow you to buy fractional shares, enabling you to invest in expensive stocks with a smaller amount of money. This feature is particularly beneficial for new investors or those with limited funds, as it provides the opportunity to invest in high-priced stocks like Amazon or Google without needing to purchase a full share.

Fractional shares make it easier to diversify your portfolio, as you can spread a smaller investment across multiple companies or ETFs.

Educational Resources

Many apps include educational content to help you improve your investment knowledge. These resources can range from articles and videos to webinars and tutorials. They cover a wide array of topics, including basic investing principles, advanced trading strategies, and market analysis.

Engaging with these educational materials can help you build confidence and enhance your investment skills, making you a more informed and effective investor.

Social and Community Features

Some investment apps incorporate social features that allow you to connect with other investors, share insights, and discuss market trends. These communities can be valuable for gaining different perspectives, learning from others' experiences, and staying motivated.

For instance, you might join a group focused on dividend investing, where members share tips and strategies for building a portfolio of dividend-paying stocks.

Security and Privacy

When using investment apps, it's crucial to ensure that your personal and financial information is secure. Most reputable apps use advanced encryption, two-factor authentication, and other security measures to protect your data. Always choose apps from well-known providers and regularly update them to benefit from the latest security features.

Cost and Fees

Investment apps typically offer low-cost trading compared to traditional brokerage firms. Some apps provide commission-free trading, while others may charge a small fee per trade or a subscription fee for premium features. It's important to understand the fee structure of any app you use to avoid unexpected costs and to choose an app that fits your budget and investment style.

Investment apps have democratized access to the financial markets, providing powerful tools and resources that can help you manage and grow your investments efficiently. Whether you are a novice investor or a seasoned trader, leveraging the features of investment apps can enhance your investment experience and support your financial goals.

Quantitative Investing: Algorithmic Trading

Algorithmic trading, also known as algo trading or automated trading, uses computer programs to execute trades based on predefined criteria and algorithms. These algorithms can analyze vast amounts of data and execute orders at speeds and frequencies far beyond human capability. This approach leverages technology to capitalize on market opportunities efficiently and accurately.

How Algorithmic Trading Works

Algorithmic trading involves using complex mathematical models and formulas to make trading decisions. Traders develop algorithms that set specific criteria for buying or selling securities. These criteria can include factors such as price, timing, volume, and other market conditions. Once these conditions are met, the algorithm automatically executes the trade.

For example, an algorithm might be programmed to buy a stock when its 50-day moving average crosses above its 200-day moving average and sell when the opposite occurs. This eliminates the emotional and psychological aspects of trading, ensuring that decisions are based solely on data and predefined rules.

Advantages of Algorithmic Trading

1. **Speed and Efficiency:** Algorithms can process and analyze data much faster than humans, allowing for rapid execution of trades. This speed is crucial in markets where prices can change in milliseconds.

2. **Accuracy:** By following predefined rules, algorithmic trading reduces the risk of human error. Trades are executed exactly as specified by the algorithm, ensuring consistency and precision.

3. **Backtesting:** Traders can backtest their algorithms against historical data to see how they would have performed in the past. This helps refine strategies and improve their potential effectiveness.

4. **Emotion-Free Trading:** Algorithms operate without emotion, which can often cloud judgment and lead to irrational decisions. This can result in more disciplined and objective trading.

5. **Cost Reduction:** Automated trading reduces the need for constant monitoring and manual intervention, potentially lowering transaction costs and operational expenses.

Types of Algorithmic Trading Strategies

1. **Trend Following:** This strategy involves identifying and following market trends. Algorithms might use moving averages, momentum indicators, or other technical analysis tools to detect trends and make trades accordingly.

2. **Arbitrage:** Arbitrage strategies exploit price differences between related securities or markets. For example, an algorithm might buy a stock on one exchange where it's

undervalued and simultaneously sell it on another exchange where it's overvalued.

3. **Market Making:** Market-making algorithms provide liquidity by continuously buying and selling securities at quoted prices. They profit from the bid-ask spread, the difference between the buying and selling prices.

4. **Mean Reversion:** This strategy assumes that asset prices will revert to their historical average over time. Algorithms identify securities that have deviated significantly from their average price and trade them in anticipation of a return to the mean.

5. **Statistical Arbitrage:** This involves using statistical models to identify and exploit pricing inefficiencies between related securities. It often involves pairs trading, where an algorithm trades two correlated assets based on the divergence in their price relationship.

Challenges and Risks

Despite its advantages, algorithmic trading also presents challenges and risks:

1. **Complexity:** Developing effective algorithms requires advanced programming skills and a deep understanding

of financial markets. Mistakes in the algorithm's design can lead to significant losses.

2. **Market Impact:** Large, rapid trades executed by algorithms can impact market prices, especially in less liquid markets. This can lead to slippage, where the trade is executed at a less favorable price than expected.

3. **Technical Failures:** Algorithmic trading systems rely on technology and infrastructure. Technical failures, such as software bugs or connectivity issues, can disrupt trading and lead to unintended consequences.

4. **Regulatory Concerns:** The use of algorithms in trading is subject to regulatory oversight. Compliance with regulations and staying updated on changes is essential to avoid legal and financial repercussions.

Implementing Algorithmic Trading

For individual investors interested in algorithmic trading, several platforms offer the necessary tools and resources. These platforms provide access to market data, backtesting capabilities, and execution services. Some popular platforms include MetaTrader, QuantConnect, and TradeStation.

To get started, investors should:

1. **Learn the Basics:** Understanding the fundamentals of algorithmic trading, including programming languages like Python and the basics of quantitative analysis, is crucial.

2. **Develop a Strategy:** Identify a trading strategy based on specific criteria and market conditions. This involves researching, testing, and refining the strategy.

3. **Backtest the Algorithm:** Use historical data to test the algorithm's performance and make necessary adjustments to improve its effectiveness.

4. **Monitor and Adjust:** Once the algorithm is live, continuously monitor its performance and make adjustments as needed to adapt to changing market conditions.

Algorithmic trading offers a powerful way to leverage technology in the financial markets. While it requires a significant investment in time and resources to develop and maintain effective algorithms, the potential benefits in terms of speed, accuracy, and efficiency make it an attractive option for sophisticated investors.

Quant Strategies

Quantitative (quant) strategies use mathematical models and statistical techniques to make investment decisions. These strategies rely on data analysis to identify trading opportunities, often leveraging complex algorithms and computer systems to execute trades with precision and speed. Here's how quant strategies work and how they can be applied to enhance your investment approach.

What Are Quant Strategies?

Quant strategies involve using quantitative analysis to guide investment decisions. This approach combines finance, mathematics, and technology to develop models that predict market movements and identify profitable trades. The core idea is to remove human emotions and biases from the investment process, relying solely on data-driven insights.

Building Quant Models

Quantitative models are built using historical market data, including price movements, trading volumes, and other financial metrics. These models are designed to identify patterns and relationships that can predict future market behavior. Key components of quant models include:

1. **Data Collection:** Gathering large amounts of historical and real-time data from various sources, such as stock exchanges, financial statements, and economic indicators.

2. **Data Analysis:** Using statistical methods and machine learning algorithms to analyze the data, identify trends, and develop predictive models.

3. **Backtesting:** Testing the models using historical data to evaluate their accuracy and performance. Backtesting helps refine the models and ensures they can generate consistent returns under different market conditions.

4. **Implementation:** Deploying the models in live trading environments, where they automatically execute trades based on predefined rules and criteria.

Types of Quant Strategies

There are several types of quant strategies, each with its own focus and methodology:

Trend Following

Trend following strategies aim to capitalize on market momentum by identifying and trading in the direction of prevailing trends. These strategies use technical indicators, such as moving averages and relative strength indices (RSI), to determine entry and exit points. For example, a trend-following model might buy a stock when its price moves above its 50-day moving average and sell when it falls below.

Mean Reversion

Mean reversion strategies are based on the idea that asset prices tend to revert to their historical averages over time. These models identify overbought or oversold conditions and execute trades anticipating a return to the mean. For instance, if a stock's price significantly deviates from its historical average, a mean reversion strategy might short the stock, expecting its price to decline back to the average.

Arbitrage

Arbitrage strategies seek to exploit price discrepancies between related assets. These models identify mispricings and execute trades to profit from the convergence of prices. Examples include statistical arbitrage, which looks for mean-reverting price relationships between securities, and merger arbitrage, which bets on the outcome of corporate mergers and acquisitions.

Factor Investing

Factor investing involves targeting specific factors, such as value, growth, or momentum, that have been shown to drive returns. Quant models identify securities that exhibit these factors and construct portfolios that maximize exposure to them. For example, a value-focused quant strategy might screen for stocks with low price-to-earnings ratios and high dividend yields.

High-Frequency Trading (HFT)

High-frequency trading uses sophisticated algorithms to execute a large number of trades at very high speeds, often within fractions of a second. HFT strategies exploit minute price discrepancies and market inefficiencies, typically requiring substantial computing power and low-latency trading infrastructure.

Benefits of Quant Strategies

1. **Data-Driven Decisions:** Quant strategies rely on objective data analysis, reducing the influence of human emotions and biases.

2. **Efficiency:** Automated trading systems can execute trades more quickly and efficiently than human traders, capturing opportunities in real-time.

3. **Consistency:** Quant models are designed to generate consistent returns by following predefined rules and criteria, ensuring disciplined investment decisions.

Challenges of Quant Strategies

1. **Complexity:** Developing and maintaining quant models requires expertise in finance, mathematics, and computer science.

2. **Data Quality:** The accuracy of quant models depends on the quality and reliability of the underlying data. Poor data can lead to incorrect predictions and losses.

3. **Market Changes:** Quant models are based on historical data, which may not always predict future market behavior. Rapid changes in market conditions can render models ineffective.

Implementing Quant Strategies

To implement quant strategies, investors can either develop their own models or invest in quant funds managed by professional firms. Developing your own models requires significant resources and expertise, while investing in quant funds allows you to leverage the skills of experienced quant managers.

Quant strategies offer a sophisticated approach to investing, leveraging data and technology to identify trading opportunities and execute trades with precision. By understanding and applying these strategies, investors can enhance their investment process and potentially achieve more consistent and robust returns.

Risk Management Techniques: Hedging Strategies

Hedging is a risk management strategy used by investors to protect against potential losses in their portfolios. By taking an offsetting position in a related security, investors can reduce the impact of adverse price movements on their investments. Understanding how to effectively use hedging strategies can help mitigate risk and provide greater stability to your portfolio.

What is Hedging?

Hedging involves making an investment that offsets potential losses in another asset. It's like taking out insurance for your investments. If the value of the primary asset declines, the hedge should generate gains that compensate for the loss.

For example, if you own a stock portfolio and are concerned about a market downturn, you might use hedging strategies to protect your investments from significant losses.

Common Hedging Strategies

1. Options

Options are a popular hedging tool. There are two main types: call options and put options.

- **Put Options:** A put option gives the holder the right to sell an asset at a predetermined price (strike price) before a specific date. If you own a stock and are worried about a price drop, buying a put option can protect you. If the stock's price falls below the strike price, the put option increases in value, offsetting the loss on the stock.

For example, if you own shares of Company XYZ at $100 each and buy a put option with a strike price of $95, if the stock falls to $85, the put option can be exercised to sell the stock at $95, minimizing your loss.

- **Call Options:** A call option gives the holder the right to buy an asset at a predetermined price. While less common as a direct hedge, call options can protect short positions. If you have shorted a stock, buying a call option can limit your potential losses if the stock price rises unexpectedly.

2. Futures Contracts

Futures contracts are agreements to buy or sell an asset at a future date for a predetermined price. They are widely used to hedge positions in commodities, currencies, and financial instruments.

For instance, a farmer growing wheat might use futures contracts to lock in the selling price of their crop months before the harvest. This protects against the risk of wheat prices falling by the time the crop is ready for market.

3. Inverse ETFs

Inverse ETFs are designed to move in the opposite direction of a specific index or asset. They can be used to hedge against market downturns. For example, if you hold a broad market ETF, you could buy shares of an inverse ETF that tracks the same index. If the market falls, the inverse ETF should increase in value, offsetting losses in the broad market ETF.

4. Currency Hedging

Investors with international exposure may face currency risk due to fluctuations in exchange rates. Currency hedging involves using financial instruments like forward contracts or currency options to protect against this risk.

For example, if you invest in European stocks but are concerned about the euro weakening against the dollar, you could enter into a forward contract to sell euros and buy dollars at a predetermined rate in the future.

Benefits of Hedging

1. **Risk Reduction:** Hedging can significantly reduce the risk of adverse price movements in your investments, providing greater portfolio stability.

2. **Peace of Mind:** Knowing that potential losses are limited can give investors more confidence and reduce the stress associated with market volatility.

3. **Enhanced Returns:** While hedging is primarily about risk reduction, it can also enhance returns by protecting investments during market downturns, ensuring a smoother performance over time.

Considerations and Risks

While hedging can protect against losses, it also has its costs and limitations. Hedging strategies can involve additional expenses, such as the premiums paid for options or the transaction costs associated with futures contracts. These costs can reduce overall returns, especially if the hedging instruments are not needed. Additionally, hedges are not always perfect, and there can be instances where the hedge does not fully offset the loss in the primary investment.

Hedging strategies are valuable tools for managing investment risk. By using options, futures, inverse ETFs, and currency hedging, investors can protect their portfolios from significant losses and navigate market volatility more effectively. Understanding the costs and potential limitations of hedging is crucial to implementing these strategies successfully.

Portfolio Insurance

Portfolio insurance is a risk management strategy designed to protect investments from significant losses during market downturns. It aims to limit downside risk while allowing for potential upside gains. Here's how portfolio insurance works and how investors can implement it effectively.

Understanding Portfolio Insurance

Portfolio insurance involves using hedging techniques to mitigate the impact of adverse market movements on a portfolio's value. The concept originated from the need to protect against catastrophic losses, especially during volatile market conditions. The primary objective is to provide downside protection without completely sacrificing potential returns.

Mechanics of Portfolio Insurance

1. **Options Strategies:** One common approach to portfolio insurance involves using options, such as put options. A put option gives the holder the right, but not the obligation, to sell a security at a predetermined price (strike price) within a specified period (expiration date). By purchasing put options on individual stocks or market indexes, investors can hedge against potential declines in their portfolio value.

2. **Dynamic Hedging:** Portfolio insurance can also employ dynamic hedging strategies. This involves continuously adjusting the portfolio's exposure to risky assets based on market conditions. For example, if the market starts to decline, the investor may increase their allocation to defensive assets or reduce exposure to equities.

3. **Stop-Loss Orders:** Another risk management tool used in portfolio insurance is stop-loss orders. A stop-loss order automatically sells a security when its price falls to a predetermined level, limiting losses. This technique is particularly useful for individual stocks but can also be applied to entire portfolios by setting stop-loss levels for ETFs or mutual funds.

Benefits of Portfolio Insurance

1. **Downside Protection:** Portfolio insurance provides a safety net against significant losses during market downturns, helping investors preserve capital.

2. **Flexibility:** There are various methods and instruments available for implementing portfolio insurance, allowing investors to customize their risk management strategies based on their risk tolerance and investment objectives.

3. **Peace of Mind:** Knowing that there is a plan in place to protect against severe market declines can reduce investor anxiety and emotional decision-making during turbulent market periods.

Considerations and Challenges

1. **Costs:** Implementing portfolio insurance using options or other hedging instruments involves costs, such as premiums for options or potential forgone gains if markets rise unexpectedly.

2. **Complexity:** Understanding and effectively implementing portfolio insurance strategies require a solid understanding of financial markets and derivatives. Investors may need professional advice or specialized knowledge to optimize these strategies.

3. **Effectiveness:** Portfolio insurance strategies are designed to mitigate losses, but they may not eliminate all risks. Market conditions can change rapidly, impacting the effectiveness of hedging techniques.

Implementing Portfolio Insurance

To implement portfolio insurance, investors should:

- **Assess Risk Tolerance:** Determine the level of risk that is acceptable and establish clear objectives for portfolio protection.

- **Select Appropriate Instruments:** Choose hedging instruments, such as put options or stop-loss orders, based on portfolio composition, market conditions, and investment horizon.

- **Regular Monitoring:** Continuously monitor market conditions and portfolio performance to adjust hedging strategies as needed. Regular reviews ensure that the insurance strategy remains aligned with investment goals.

Portfolio insurance is a proactive approach to managing investment risk, offering investors a way to safeguard their portfolios against potential downturns while maintaining exposure to growth opportunities. By understanding the mechanics and considerations of portfolio insurance, investors can make informed decisions to protect and enhance their investment portfolios.

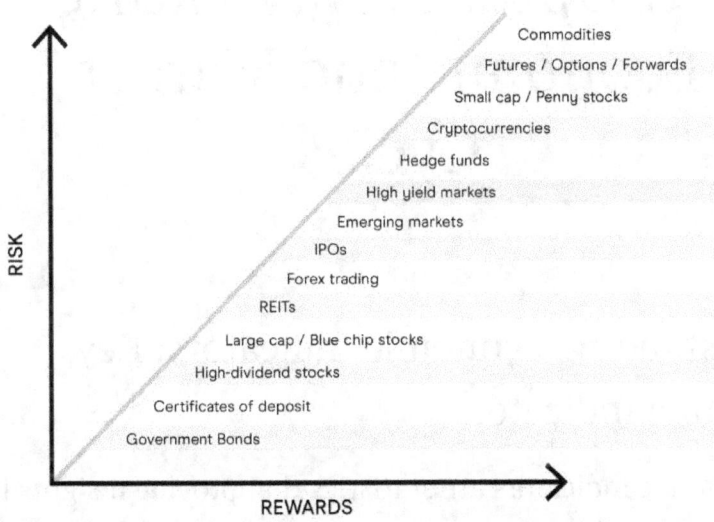

Risk/Reward Ratio. Source: cmcmarkets.com

Chapter 8: Navigating Economic and Market Cycles

Understanding Economic Indicators: Key Economic Indicators

Key economic indicators are statistics that provide insights into the health and direction of an economy. Investors and policymakers closely monitor these indicators to gauge economic performance, predict future trends, and make informed decisions. Understanding these indicators is crucial for assessing the overall economic environment and its potential impact on investment markets.

Gross Domestic Product (GDP)

GDP measures the total value of goods and services produced within a country's borders over a specific period, typically quarterly or annually. It serves as a broad indicator of economic activity and growth. A rising GDP generally indicates a growing economy, while a declining GDP may signal economic contraction.

Unemployment Rate

The unemployment rate measures the percentage of the labor force that is actively seeking employment but currently unemployed. Low unemployment rates suggest a strong labor market and potential wage pressures, which can influence consumer spending and economic growth.

Inflation Rate

The inflation rate measures the rate at which the general level of prices for goods and services is rising. Moderate inflation is often viewed positively as it reflects economic expansion. However, high or rapidly increasing inflation can erode purchasing power and lead to economic instability.

Consumer Price Index (CPI)

The CPI is a measure of the average change over time in the prices paid by urban consumers for a basket of goods and services. It is a key indicator of inflationary trends and is used to adjust income and pensions for changes in the cost of living.

Interest Rates

Interest rates, set by central banks, influence borrowing costs for businesses and consumers. Lower interest rates can stimulate economic growth by making borrowing cheaper, while higher rates can curb inflation but may slow economic activity.

Trade Balance

The trade balance measures the difference between a country's exports and imports of goods and services. A positive trade balance (surplus) indicates that a country exports more than it imports, contributing positively to GDP growth. A negative trade balance (deficit) suggests the opposite and may impact currency exchange rates.

Consumer Confidence Index (CCI)

The CCI reflects consumers' optimism about the state of the economy, employment opportunities, and their personal financial situation. High consumer confidence often correlates with increased consumer spending, which drives economic growth.

Business Confidence Index (BCI)

The BCI measures business leaders' optimism about economic conditions and their outlook for future business performance. High business confidence can lead to increased investment, hiring, and economic expansion.

Housing Market Indicators

Indicators such as housing starts, home sales, and home price indices provide insights into the health of the housing market, a critical sector of the economy. Strength in the housing market often reflects consumer confidence and contributes to economic growth through construction activity and related spending.

Stock Market Indices

Stock market indices, such as the S&P 500 or Dow Jones Industrial Average, track the performance of a basket of stocks. They are used as indicators of overall market sentiment and can reflect investor confidence and expectations about future economic conditions.

Labor Productivity

Labor productivity measures the output per hour worked and is an indicator of economic efficiency and growth potential. Higher productivity levels can support higher wages and living standards over time.

Key economic indicators provide valuable insights into the economic landscape, helping investors, policymakers, and businesses make informed decisions. By monitoring these indicators regularly and understanding their implications, stakeholders can navigate economic cycles and adapt strategies to capitalize on opportunities and manage risks effectively.

How They Affect Investments

Economic indicators are essential tools for investors as they provide insights into the current and future state of the economy. Understanding how these indicators affect investments can help investors make more informed decisions and better manage their portfolios.

Gross Domestic Product (GDP)

GDP growth indicates a healthy and expanding economy, which is generally positive for investments. When GDP is rising, businesses are likely experiencing higher sales and profits, leading to higher stock prices. Conversely, declining GDP suggests economic contraction, which can result in lower corporate earnings and falling stock prices. Investors often look to GDP reports to gauge overall economic health and adjust their investment strategies accordingly.

Unemployment Rate

The unemployment rate influences consumer spending, which drives a significant portion of economic activity. Low unemployment typically means more people have jobs and disposable income, leading to increased consumer spending and higher corporate revenues. This is usually positive for the stock market. High unemployment, on the other hand, can reduce consumer spending, negatively affecting businesses and their stock prices. Bond investors may see high unemployment as a sign of economic weakness, potentially leading to lower interest rates.

Inflation Rate

Moderate inflation is generally seen as a sign of a growing economy, but high inflation can erode purchasing power and squeeze profit margins. For stock investors, high inflation can lead to higher input costs for companies, reducing profitability. Bonds are particularly sensitive to inflation because it erodes the fixed interest payments they provide. High inflation often leads to higher interest rates, which can decrease bond prices.

Consumer Price Index (CPI)

The CPI is closely watched as it measures inflation at the consumer level. Rising CPI indicates increasing inflation, which can lead to higher interest rates and lower bond prices. For stocks, a rising CPI can be a double-edged sword: it might signal strong consumer demand, but it also suggests higher costs for businesses. Companies that can pass on higher costs to consumers might fare better than those that cannot.

Interest Rates

Interest rates set by central banks have a significant impact on all types of investments. When interest rates are low, borrowing costs decrease, encouraging businesses to invest and expand.

This is generally positive for stock markets. Low interest rates also make bonds less attractive, as their fixed returns are less competitive compared to potential stock returns. Conversely, high interest rates can slow economic growth by increasing borrowing costs, which can negatively affect stock prices. However, higher rates make bonds more attractive to investors seeking stable returns.

Trade Balance

A country's trade balance affects currency values and economic health. A trade surplus (more exports than imports) can strengthen a country's currency and stimulate economic growth, which is positive for domestic stocks. A trade deficit (more imports than exports) might weaken the currency and signal economic issues, potentially leading to lower stock prices. Changes in the trade balance can also impact specific sectors, such as exporters and importers.

Consumer Confidence Index (CCI)

High consumer confidence typically leads to increased consumer spending, benefiting companies and their stock prices. Investors monitor the CCI to predict spending trends and make investment decisions based on expected consumer behavior. Low consumer confidence can signal reduced spending, negatively impacting businesses, especially those in the retail and consumer goods sectors.

Business Confidence Index (BCI)

The BCI reflects the outlook of business leaders on economic conditions. High business confidence can lead to increased investment, expansion, and hiring, positively affecting the stock market. Low business confidence might indicate economic uncertainty, leading companies to delay investments or cut costs, which can hurt stock prices. Investors use the BCI to gauge the business environment and adjust their portfolios accordingly.

Housing Market Indicators

Strong housing market indicators, such as rising home sales and prices, suggest economic growth and consumer confidence. This can boost related sectors like construction, home improvement, and real estate. For investors, positive housing data can be a signal to invest in these sectors. Weak housing data, however, can indicate economic troubles, affecting stocks tied to the housing market.

Stock Market Indices

Stock market indices reflect overall market sentiment and economic conditions. Rising indices suggest investor confidence and economic growth, encouraging further investment. Falling indices may indicate economic concerns and lead to reduced investment. Investors use these indices to assess market trends and adjust their strategies accordingly.

Labor Productivity

Higher labor productivity means that the economy can produce more goods and services with the same amount of labor, leading to higher economic growth and potentially higher stock prices. Companies that improve productivity can increase their profitability, making their stocks more attractive to investors.

Economic indicators provide valuable insights that help investors understand the broader economic context and its impact on various asset classes. By analyzing these indicators, investors can better anticipate market movements and make strategic investment decisions to optimize their portfolios.

Market Cycles and Trends: Bull and Bear Markets

Bull and bear markets are terms used to describe the overall direction and sentiment of financial markets. Understanding these market conditions is essential for making informed investment decisions and managing your portfolio effectively.

Bull Markets

A bull market is characterized by rising asset prices and widespread investor confidence. During a bull market, the economy is generally strong, unemployment rates are low, and consumer spending is robust. Investors are optimistic, and the demand for stocks, real estate, and other assets drives prices higher.

Characteristics of a Bull Market

1. **Rising Prices:** One of the most obvious signs of a bull market is a sustained increase in asset prices, particularly in the stock market. This upward trend can last for months or even years.

2. **Investor Confidence:** Optimism prevails among investors, who are willing to buy stocks and other assets, expecting future gains. Positive economic news and corporate earnings reports often fuel this confidence.

3. **Economic Growth:** Bull markets typically coincide with periods of strong economic growth. Key economic indicators such as GDP, employment rates, and consumer spending show positive trends.

4. **Increased IPO Activity:** During bull markets, companies are more likely to go public, seeking to capitalize on high investor demand and favorable market conditions.

Investing in a Bull Market

During a bull market, investors often seek to maximize their gains by investing in growth stocks, which are expected to outperform the broader market. It's also common to see increased participation in the market, as rising prices attract new investors.

Bear Markets

A bear market is the opposite of a bull market, characterized by falling asset prices and pervasive investor pessimism. During a bear market, the economy may be weakening, unemployment rates might be rising, and consumer spending can decline. Investors become cautious, leading to a decrease in demand for stocks and other assets, which pushes prices lower.

Characteristics of a Bear Market

1. **Falling Prices:** A bear market is marked by a sustained decline in asset prices, particularly in the stock market. This downward trend can also last for months or years.

2. **Investor Pessimism:** Investors are generally pessimistic, selling off assets to avoid further losses. Negative economic news and disappointing corporate earnings reports contribute to this sentiment.

3. **Economic Contraction:** Bear markets often occur during periods of economic contraction or recession. Key economic indicators such as GDP, employment rates, and consumer spending show negative trends.

4. **Increased Volatility:** Bear markets tend to be more volatile, with larger and more frequent price swings. This increased uncertainty can make it challenging for investors to predict market movements.

Investing in a Bear Market

During a bear market, investors might focus on preserving capital and reducing risk. Strategies such as shifting investments to safer assets like bonds, holding cash, or investing in defensive stocks that tend to perform well during economic downturns can help mitigate losses.

Identifying Market Trends

Recognizing the signs of bull and bear markets can help investors adjust their strategies accordingly. While no one can predict market movements with certainty, staying informed about economic indicators, corporate earnings, and global events can provide valuable insights.

For example, a prolonged period of rising stock prices, coupled with strong economic data and high investor confidence, likely indicates a bull market. Conversely, a sustained decline in stock prices, weak economic data, and low investor confidence suggest a bear market.

Psychological Factors

Investor psychology plays a significant role in bull and bear markets. During bull markets, the fear of missing out (FOMO) can drive prices higher as more investors buy in. In bear markets, fear and panic selling can exacerbate price declines.

Understanding these psychological factors can help investors maintain a long-term perspective and avoid making impulsive decisions based on short-term market movements. It's essential to stay disciplined, stick to your investment plan, and adjust your portfolio based on your risk tolerance and financial goals rather than reacting to market emotions.

Identifying Market Trends

Identifying market trends is crucial for making informed investment decisions. Market trends reflect the general direction in which the market or a particular asset is moving over a specific period. Understanding these trends can help investors anticipate changes and adjust their portfolios accordingly.

Types of Market Trends

There are three primary types of market trends: upward (bullish), downward (bearish), and sideways (neutral).

Upward (Bullish) Trends

An upward trend occurs when the prices of securities consistently rise over time. Bullish trends are characterized by higher highs and higher lows. Investors in a bullish market are generally optimistic, expecting prices to continue rising. Indicators of a bullish trend include:

- Strong economic data, such as GDP growth and low unemployment rates.
- Positive corporate earnings reports.
- High consumer confidence and spending.
- Increasing stock market indices.

For example, during an economic expansion, companies often experience higher revenues and profits, leading to rising stock prices and a bullish market trend.

Downward (Bearish) Trends

A downward trend is when the prices of securities consistently fall over time. Bearish trends are marked by lower highs and lower lows. Investors in a bearish market are generally pessimistic, expecting prices to continue declining. Indicators of a bearish trend include:

- Weak economic data, such as declining GDP and rising unemployment.

- Negative corporate earnings reports.

- Low consumer confidence and spending.

- Decreasing stock market indices.

During a recession, for instance, reduced consumer spending and business investment can lead to declining corporate earnings and falling stock prices, resulting in a bearish market trend.

Sideways (Neutral) Trends

A sideways trend occurs when prices move within a horizontal range, showing no clear upward or downward direction. These trends indicate market indecision, where neither bulls nor bears dominate. Indicators of a sideways trend include:

- Mixed economic data.

- Stable corporate earnings with no significant growth or decline.

- Balanced investor sentiment.

Sideways trends can be seen during periods of market consolidation, where prices stabilize after a significant move up or down, as investors await new information to determine the next direction.

Tools for Identifying Trends

Investors use various tools and techniques to identify market trends, including technical analysis, fundamental analysis, and sentiment analysis.

Technical Analysis

Technical analysis involves studying price charts and using indicators to identify patterns and trends. Common tools include:

- Moving Averages: These smooth out price data to help identify the direction of the trend. A rising moving average indicates an upward trend, while a falling moving average indicates a downward trend.

- Trendlines: Drawing lines along the highs and lows of price movements can help visualize the trend direction.

- Relative Strength Index (RSI): This momentum indicator measures the speed and change of price movements, helping to identify overbought or oversold conditions.

For example, if a stock's price is consistently above its 50-day moving average, it suggests an upward trend.

Fundamental Analysis

Fundamental analysis involves evaluating economic indicators, financial statements, and other qualitative and quantitative factors to determine the intrinsic value of an asset. Key factors include:

- Economic Indicators: GDP growth, unemployment rates, and inflation can provide insights into market trends.

- Corporate Earnings: Strong earnings growth can indicate a potential upward trend, while declining earnings might suggest a downward trend.

- Industry Analysis: Understanding industry trends and competitive dynamics can help identify broader market trends.

For instance, if a company reports consistently strong earnings growth and positive future guidance, it might indicate an upward trend in its stock price.

Sentiment Analysis

Sentiment analysis gauges investor mood and market psychology. Tools for sentiment analysis include:

- Surveys: Surveys like the Consumer Confidence Index (CCI) and the American Association of Individual Investors (AAII) Sentiment Survey provide insights into investor sentiment.

- Market Volume: High trading volumes during price increases can indicate bullish sentiment, while high volumes during price declines can indicate bearish sentiment.

- News and Social Media: Analyzing news articles, financial reports, and social media trends can provide insights into market sentiment.

For example, widespread optimism in news headlines and social media discussions about a particular sector might indicate a bullish trend in that sector.

Applying Trend Analysis

Once you've identified the current market trend, you can adjust your investment strategy accordingly. In an upward trend, you might increase your exposure to growth-oriented assets like stocks. In a downward trend, you might shift towards defensive assets like bonds or consider short-selling opportunities. During sideways trends, you might focus on assets with stable returns or look for breakout opportunities.

Identifying market trends involves analyzing various indicators and using different tools to understand the market's direction. By recognizing these trends, investors can make more informed decisions, optimize their portfolios, and better navigate market cycles.

Adapting to Changing Markets: Flexible Investment Strategies

Flexible investment strategies are essential for adapting to changing market conditions and achieving long-term financial goals. These strategies allow investors to adjust their portfolios based on market trends, economic indicators, and personal circumstances. Here's how to implement flexible investment strategies effectively.

Diversification

Diversification is a key component of a flexible investment strategy. By spreading investments across various asset classes, sectors, and geographic regions, you can reduce risk and increase the potential for returns. A well-diversified portfolio might include stocks, bonds, real estate, and alternative investments such as commodities or cryptocurrencies. This approach helps cushion the impact of poor performance in any single asset class.

Asset Allocation Adjustments

Adjusting asset allocation in response to market conditions is another crucial aspect of flexibility. For example, during periods of economic growth, you might increase your exposure to equities to take advantage of rising stock prices. Conversely, during economic downturns, shifting more assets into bonds or cash can help protect your portfolio from significant losses.

Tactical Asset Allocation

Tactical asset allocation involves making short-term adjustments to your portfolio based on market conditions and economic outlook. This strategy requires regular monitoring and a willingness to act on new information. For instance, if you anticipate a sector, such as technology or healthcare, to outperform, you might temporarily increase your investment in that sector.

Rebalancing

Regularly rebalancing your portfolio ensures that your asset allocation remains aligned with your investment goals and risk tolerance. Market fluctuations can cause your portfolio to drift from its original allocation. Rebalancing involves selling overperforming assets and buying underperforming ones to maintain your desired asset mix.

Using Stop-Loss Orders

Stop-loss orders can be an effective tool for managing risk and protecting your investments. A stop-loss order automatically sells a security when its price falls to a predetermined level, limiting potential losses. This strategy can be particularly useful during volatile market periods, helping you avoid significant downturns.

Income and Growth Balance

Balancing income and growth in your portfolio can provide both stability and potential for capital appreciation. Investing in dividend-paying stocks or bonds can offer a steady income stream, while growth stocks and real estate investments can provide opportunities for long-term appreciation. Adjusting this balance based on market conditions and personal financial needs ensures a more flexible approach.

Staying Informed

Keeping abreast of market trends, economic indicators, and geopolitical events is essential for implementing flexible investment strategies. Staying informed allows you to make timely adjustments to your portfolio and take advantage of new opportunities or mitigate emerging risks.

Adapting to Life Changes

Your personal circumstances and financial goals may change over time, necessitating adjustments to your investment strategy. Major life events such as marriage, the birth of a child, or retirement planning can impact your risk tolerance and investment horizon. Regularly reviewing and updating your strategy ensures it remains aligned with your current situation and future objectives.

Risk Management

Managing risk is a critical component of flexible investment strategies. This includes diversifying investments, using hedging techniques, and setting stop-loss orders. Additionally, maintaining a portion of your portfolio in cash or liquid assets can provide a buffer during market downturns and offer the flexibility to take advantage of new investment opportunities.

Long-Term Perspective

While flexibility is important, maintaining a long-term perspective helps you avoid reacting impulsively to short-term market fluctuations. Staying focused on your long-term goals and adjusting your strategy based on well-founded analysis rather than market noise can lead to more consistent and successful investment outcomes.

Flexible investment strategies enable you to navigate various market conditions and adjust your portfolio to meet your evolving financial goals. By incorporating diversification, tactical asset allocation, regular rebalancing, and staying informed, you can create a resilient and adaptive investment approach.

Staying Ahead of the Curve

Staying ahead of the curve in investing means anticipating market changes and adjusting your strategies proactively. This proactive approach can help you capitalize on opportunities and mitigate risks, ensuring your portfolio remains resilient through various market conditions.

Continuous Learning

The investment landscape is constantly evolving, influenced by economic shifts, technological advancements, and geopolitical events. To stay ahead, commit to continuous learning. Regularly read financial news, follow market analysis, and study investment literature. Engaging with diverse sources of information helps you understand emerging trends and develop a broader perspective.

For example, reading industry reports and financial journals can provide insights into technological innovations that might impact specific sectors, allowing you to invest early in promising companies.

Leveraging Technology

Utilize technology to gain an edge in the market. Investment apps, online platforms, and financial software offer tools for real-time data analysis, portfolio management, and trading. Algorithms and artificial intelligence can analyze vast amounts of data quickly, identifying patterns and opportunities that might not be immediately apparent.

For instance, using a portfolio management app can help you track your investments, analyze performance, and rebalance your portfolio efficiently based on current market conditions.

Networking and Professional Advice

Building a network of knowledgeable professionals can provide valuable insights and advice. Attend industry conferences, join investment clubs, and participate in online forums to connect with other investors and experts. Networking can expose you to different viewpoints and strategies, enriching your investment approach.

Additionally, seeking advice from financial advisors or investment professionals can help you make informed decisions. Advisors can provide tailored strategies based on your financial goals and risk tolerance, helping you navigate complex market environments.

Diversification

Diversification is a fundamental strategy for staying ahead of the curve. By spreading your investments across various asset classes, sectors, and geographic regions, you can reduce risk and enhance returns. Diversified portfolios are more resilient to market volatility and can capitalize on opportunities in different areas.

For example, if you have investments in technology stocks, real estate, bonds, and international markets, your portfolio is less likely to suffer significant losses from a downturn in any single sector.

-

Monitoring Economic Indicators

Regularly monitor key economic indicators such as GDP growth, unemployment rates, inflation, and interest rates. These indicators provide insights into the overall health of the economy and can signal potential market shifts. Understanding how these metrics impact different asset classes helps you adjust your investment strategy accordingly.

For instance, if economic indicators suggest rising inflation, you might consider investing in assets that typically perform well in inflationary environments, such as commodities or inflation-protected securities.

Staying Flexible and Adaptable

Markets are dynamic, and rigid strategies can lead to missed opportunities or increased risks. Stay flexible and be willing to adapt your investment approach as conditions change. This might involve rebalancing your portfolio, shifting focus to different sectors, or adjusting your risk exposure.

For example, during periods of economic uncertainty, you might reduce exposure to high-risk stocks and increase holdings in defensive assets like bonds or dividend-paying stocks.

Scenario Planning

Engage in scenario planning to prepare for various market outcomes. Consider different scenarios, such as economic booms, recessions, or geopolitical events, and develop strategies for each. Scenario planning helps you anticipate potential risks and opportunities, making you better prepared to respond effectively.

For instance, you might develop a plan for a potential market downturn that includes steps like increasing cash reserves, investing in stable assets, or identifying undervalued stocks for potential recovery investments.

Reviewing and Adjusting Strategies

Regularly review your investment strategies and performance. Set aside time to analyze your portfolio, assess the effectiveness of your strategies, and make necessary adjustments. Continuous evaluation ensures your investments align with your goals and adapt to changing market conditions.

For example, conducting quarterly reviews of your portfolio can help you identify underperforming assets, adjust allocations, and incorporate new investment opportunities based on the latest market trends.

Staying ahead of the curve in investing involves continuous learning, leveraging technology, networking, diversification, and adaptability. By proactively monitoring the market and being prepared to adjust your strategies, you can better navigate the complexities of investing and achieve your financial objectives.

Chapter 9: Building a Sustainable Investment Portfolio

Principles of Sustainable Investing: ESG Criteria (Environmental, Social, Governance)

ESG criteria refer to Environmental, Social, and Governance factors that investors use to evaluate the sustainability and ethical impact of an investment in a company or business. Incorporating ESG criteria into your investment strategy can help align your portfolio with your values while potentially enhancing long-term returns by identifying companies that are well-positioned for sustainable growth.

Environmental Criteria

Environmental criteria consider how a company performs as a steward of nature. This includes how it manages resources, reduces waste, and addresses climate change. Key areas of focus include:

- **Carbon Footprint:** Assessing the company's greenhouse gas emissions and efforts to reduce them. Companies that actively work to lower their carbon footprint can mitigate risks associated with climate change and regulatory pressures.

- **Resource Management:** Evaluating how efficiently a company uses natural resources such as water, energy, and raw materials. Sustainable resource management can lead to cost savings and reduce environmental impact.

- **Pollution and Waste:** Analyzing the company's waste management practices, including its efforts to minimize pollution and improve waste recycling and disposal. Companies with robust pollution control measures can avoid legal liabilities and reputational damage.

For example, investing in a company that has committed to using renewable energy sources and has implemented a comprehensive plan to reduce emissions demonstrates strong environmental stewardship.

Social Criteria

Social criteria examine how a company manages relationships with its employees, suppliers, customers, and communities.

This includes its commitment to human rights, labor standards, and community engagement. Important aspects include:

- **Labor Practices:** Investigating how a company treats its workforce, including fair wages, safe working conditions, and benefits. Companies with strong labor practices can attract and retain talent, enhancing productivity and morale.

- **Diversity and Inclusion:** Assessing the company's efforts to promote diversity and inclusion within its workforce and leadership. A diverse and inclusive workplace can drive innovation and reflect the company's adaptability to a global market.

- **Community Impact:** Considering the company's contributions to the communities in which it operates, including charitable activities and local economic support. Positive community engagement can build strong local relationships and enhance the company's reputation.

For instance, a company known for its inclusive workplace policies and active community involvement may be seen as a positive social investment.

Governance Criteria

Governance criteria focus on how a company is governed and its corporate behavior. This includes transparency, board diversity, executive compensation, and shareholder rights. Critical governance factors include:

- **Board Structure:** Examining the composition and independence of the board of directors. A diverse and independent board can provide better oversight and decision-making.

- **Transparency and Accountability:** Evaluating the company's financial disclosures and commitment to transparent reporting. Companies that are transparent and accountable to shareholders can build trust and reduce the risk of fraud or mismanagement.

- **Ethical Conduct:** Reviewing the company's adherence to ethical business practices and regulatory compliance. Ethical conduct can prevent legal issues and enhance the company's long-term viability.

For example, a company with a transparent governance structure, including clear reporting practices and ethical guidelines, can be a more attractive investment for those concerned with corporate integrity.

Incorporating ESG Criteria into Investing

Incorporating ESG criteria into your investment decisions involves researching and selecting companies that meet high standards in these areas. Many investors use ESG ratings and reports provided by independent agencies to assess companies' performance on these criteria. Additionally, ESG-focused mutual funds and ETFs allow investors to invest in a diversified portfolio of companies that meet specific ESG standards.

Benefits of ESG Investing

ESG investing can offer several benefits, including:

- **Risk Mitigation:** Companies with strong ESG practices are often better equipped to manage risks related to environmental regulations, social dynamics, and governance issues.

- **Long-Term Performance:** Evidence suggests that companies with robust ESG practices can achieve better long-term financial performance due to sustainable practices and improved risk management.

- **Alignment with Values:** ESG investing allows investors to align their portfolios with their ethical values and contribute to positive social and environmental outcomes.

By integrating ESG criteria into your investment strategy, you can pursue financial returns while supporting companies that contribute to a more sustainable and equitable world. This approach can help build a resilient portfolio that aligns with your personal values and long-term investment goals.

ESG Criteria. Source: anevis-solutions.com

Impact Investing

Impact investing is an investment approach that aims to generate positive social and environmental effects alongside financial returns. This strategy focuses on supporting companies, organizations, and projects that address societal challenges while providing investors with a return on their investment. Here's a closer look at what impact investing entails and how it can be integrated into your investment strategy.

Defining Impact Investing

Impact investing goes beyond traditional investment objectives by intentionally targeting investments that make a measurable positive impact on society or the environment. These investments can span various sectors, including renewable energy, affordable housing, healthcare, education, and sustainable agriculture.

Key Characteristics

Impact investing involves several key characteristics:

1. **Intentionality:** Investors intentionally seek to generate social or environmental benefits in addition to financial

returns. This intention is a defining feature that distinguishes impact investing from other forms of socially responsible investing (SRI).

2. **Measurability:** Impact investments are designed to achieve measurable outcomes. Investors use specific metrics and reporting standards to assess the social and environmental performance of their investments.

3. **Financial Returns:** Impact investments aim to provide financial returns that can range from below-market to market-rate, depending on the goals and risk tolerance of the investor.

Examples of Impact Investments

There are various ways to engage in impact investing:

1. **Renewable Energy Projects:** Investing in companies or projects that develop and promote clean energy sources, such as solar, wind, and hydroelectric power. These investments contribute to reducing carbon emissions and combating climate change.

2. **Affordable Housing:** Funding projects that provide affordable housing solutions for low-income families and

individuals. These investments help address housing shortages and improve living conditions.

3. **Healthcare Innovations:** Supporting companies that develop innovative healthcare solutions, including affordable medical treatments, telemedicine, and health technologies that improve access to care.

4. **Education Initiatives:** Investing in educational technologies, schools, and programs that enhance learning opportunities and outcomes for underserved populations.

Evaluating Impact Investments

To effectively engage in impact investing, it's essential to evaluate potential investments based on their social and environmental impact, as well as their financial performance. Here are some steps to consider:

1. **Identify Impact Goals:** Determine the specific social or environmental issues you want to address through your investments. This could include areas like poverty alleviation, clean energy, education, or healthcare.

2. **Research Investment Opportunities:** Look for investment opportunities that align with your impact

goals. This might involve exploring mutual funds, ETFs, private equity, or direct investments in companies and projects.

3. **Assess Impact Metrics:** Evaluate how the investment measures and reports its impact. Look for investments that use standardized impact metrics and reporting frameworks, such as the Global Impact Investing Network's (GIIN) Impact Reporting and Investment Standards (IRIS).

4. **Analyze Financial Performance:** Consider the financial performance and risk profile of the investment. Impact investments should balance social and environmental benefits with the potential for financial returns.

Benefits of Impact Investing

Impact investing offers several benefits:

1. **Positive Social and Environmental Impact:** Impact investments directly contribute to addressing global challenges and improving societal well-being.

2. **Alignment with Values:** Investors can align their portfolios with their personal values and ethical beliefs, supporting causes they care about.

3. **Portfolio Diversification:** Impact investments can diversify an investment portfolio, potentially reducing risk and enhancing long-term returns.

4. **Potential for Innovation:** Impact investments often support innovative solutions and emerging industries, offering growth opportunities.

Challenges and Considerations

While impact investing has many advantages, it also presents challenges:

1. **Measuring Impact:** Quantifying the social and environmental impact of investments can be complex and may require specialized knowledge and resources.

2. **Financial Trade-offs:** Some impact investments may offer lower financial returns compared to traditional investments. Investors need to balance their impact goals with their financial objectives.

3. **Limited Availability:** Finding suitable impact investment opportunities can be challenging, as the market is still developing and may have limited options compared to traditional investments.

Impact investing is a powerful approach that enables investors to generate positive social and environmental outcomes while achieving financial returns. By carefully selecting and evaluating impact investments, you can build a portfolio that reflects your values and contributes to a more sustainable and equitable world.

Strategies for Sustainable Investing: Selecting the Right Investments

Selecting sustainable investments involves identifying companies and funds that meet high standards for environmental, social, and governance (ESG) practices. This process can help you build a portfolio that aligns with your values and supports long-term, responsible growth. Here's how to approach selecting sustainable investments effectively.

Define Your Values and Goals

Begin by clearly defining what sustainability means to you and what specific ESG criteria are most important. Consider whether you prioritize environmental issues like climate change and renewable energy, social issues such as labor practices and community impact, or governance factors like transparency and ethical conduct.

For example, if climate change is a primary concern, you might focus on companies that are leaders in renewable energy or those with aggressive carbon reduction goals.

Research and Evaluate Companies

Thoroughly research potential investments to evaluate their ESG practices. Look for companies that demonstrate a strong commitment to sustainability in their operations and policies. Key areas to examine include:

- **Environmental Impact:** Assess the company's initiatives to reduce its carbon footprint, manage natural resources, and minimize waste and pollution. Companies with comprehensive sustainability programs and clear environmental goals are often more attractive investments.

- **Social Responsibility:** Evaluate the company's treatment of employees, commitment to diversity and inclusion, and impact on local communities. Companies that prioritize fair labor practices, support community development, and foster inclusive workplaces tend to perform better over the long term.

- **Governance Practices:** Review the company's governance structure, including board diversity, executive compensation, and transparency in reporting. Strong governance practices can enhance a company's stability and resilience.

Many companies provide detailed ESG reports that outline their sustainability initiatives and achievements. Additionally, third-party ESG ratings and research reports can offer valuable insights into a company's performance.

Use ESG Ratings and Indices

Several organizations provide ESG ratings and indices that rank companies based on their sustainability performance. These ratings can be a helpful tool in identifying companies that meet your ESG criteria. Common ESG rating agencies include MSCI, Sustainalytics, and FTSE Russell.

For example, the MSCI ESG Ratings evaluate companies on a scale from AAA to CCC based on their exposure to ESG risks and their ability to manage those risks. Higher-rated companies are considered better at handling ESG issues, making them potentially more sustainable investments.

Consider ESG-Focused Funds

Investing in ESG-focused mutual funds or exchange-traded funds (ETFs) is a practical way to gain exposure to a diversified portfolio of sustainable investments. These funds typically select companies based on specific ESG criteria and can provide an efficient way to align your investments with your values.

Look for funds with a strong track record of performance and a clear investment strategy focused on sustainability. Review the fund's holdings to ensure they align with your specific ESG priorities.

Engage with Companies

As an investor, you have the power to influence corporate behavior through shareholder engagement. This can involve voting on shareholder resolutions related to ESG issues, participating in annual meetings, or engaging in dialogue with company management to advocate for sustainable practices.

By actively engaging with companies, you can encourage better ESG performance and support initiatives that drive long-term value creation.

Monitor and Review Investments

Sustainable investing is an ongoing process. Regularly monitor your investments to ensure they continue to meet your ESG criteria and perform well financially. Stay informed about developments in ESG practices and adjust your portfolio as needed to align with evolving goals and market conditions.

Reviewing annual ESG reports and staying updated on news related to your investments can help you make informed decisions and maintain a sustainable portfolio.

Selecting sustainable investments involves careful research, the use of reliable ESG ratings, and active engagement with companies. By following these steps, you can build a portfolio that supports your values, contributes to positive social and environmental outcomes, and achieves long-term financial success.

Balancing Returns and Impact

Balancing financial returns with social and environmental impact is a core principle of sustainable investing. Investors who seek to achieve this balance aim to generate competitive financial returns while supporting initiatives that promote positive change. This approach requires thoughtful strategy and careful selection of investments.

Defining Your Objectives

To balance returns and impact, start by clearly defining your financial goals and impact objectives. Determine what level of financial return you need to meet your personal or institutional goals and identify the social or environmental issues you are passionate about addressing. This clarity helps in selecting investments that align with both your financial and impact targets.

Assessing Investment Opportunities

When evaluating potential investments, consider both their financial performance and their impact potential. Look for companies or funds that have a proven track record of achieving both strong financial returns and measurable positive impacts.

1. **Financial Performance:** Analyze traditional financial metrics such as revenue growth, profitability, and return on investment. Ensure that the investment meets your expected financial criteria.

2. **Impact Measurement:** Review how the investment measures and reports its social or environmental impact.

Investments with clear, transparent impact metrics and reporting practices are preferable.

Integrating ESG Factors

Incorporate environmental, social, and governance (ESG) factors into your investment analysis. ESG integration involves evaluating how a company's operations and policies affect the environment, society, and governance. Companies with strong ESG practices are often better managed and less likely to face legal or reputational risks, potentially leading to better long-term financial performance.

For example, a company with robust environmental policies might be more sustainable in the long run, reducing costs and risks associated with environmental regulations. Similarly, a company with strong governance practices is less likely to encounter issues like fraud or management scandals.

Diversifying Your Portfolio

Diversification is key to balancing returns and impact. Spread your investments across various asset classes, sectors, and geographic regions to reduce risk. Include a mix of impact-focused investments and traditional investments to achieve a balanced portfolio.

For instance, you might allocate a portion of your portfolio to green bonds, which finance environmentally friendly projects, while also investing in companies with strong ESG ratings in different industries. This approach allows you to support impactful initiatives without compromising financial stability.

Active vs. Passive Management

Decide whether you want an actively managed or passively managed approach to sustainable investing. Actively managed funds involve portfolio managers making specific investment decisions to achieve both financial returns and impact goals. These funds can adapt quickly to changing market conditions and emerging impact opportunities.

Passively managed funds, such as ESG-focused index funds, aim to replicate the performance of a market index while incorporating ESG criteria. These funds typically have lower fees and can provide broad market exposure with an impact focus.

Engaging with Companies

As an investor, you have the power to influence corporate behavior through shareholder engagement. Engage with the companies you invest in by voting on shareholder resolutions, attending annual meetings, and participating in dialogues with management. Encourage companies to adopt more sustainable practices and improve their ESG performance.

For example, you might advocate for a company to reduce its carbon footprint, improve labor practices, or enhance board diversity. Active engagement can drive meaningful changes that align with your impact goals.

Monitoring and Adjusting Your Strategy

Regularly monitor the performance of your investments to ensure they are meeting both financial and impact objectives. Review financial statements, impact reports, and market trends. Be prepared to adjust your strategy as needed based on changing market conditions or new opportunities.

If an investment consistently underperforms financially or fails to achieve its impact goals, consider rebalancing your portfolio to better align with your objectives.

Balancing returns and impact in sustainable investing requires a thoughtful and strategic approach. By defining clear objectives, assessing opportunities, integrating ESG factors, diversifying your portfolio, and engaging with companies, you can achieve a harmonious blend of financial success and positive societal contributions. Regular monitoring and adjustments ensure that your investment strategy remains aligned with your evolving goals and market dynamics.

The Future of Sustainable Investing: Trends and Innovations

Sustainable investing is continually evolving, driven by new trends and innovations that shape how investors approach environmental, social, and governance (ESG) criteria. Staying informed about these developments can help you make more informed investment decisions and capitalize on emerging opportunities.

Increased Focus on Climate Change

One of the most significant trends in sustainable investing is the growing focus on climate change. Investors are increasingly aware of the financial risks associated with global warming and the transition to a low-carbon economy. This has led to a surge in demand for investments that support environmental sustainability.

Companies that actively work to reduce their carbon footprints, adopt renewable energy sources, and improve energy efficiency are becoming more attractive to investors. Additionally, financial products like green bonds, which fund environmentally friendly projects, are gaining popularity.

Advancements in ESG Data and Analytics

The availability and quality of ESG data have improved significantly, thanks to advancements in technology and data analytics. Sophisticated tools and platforms now provide investors with detailed insights into a company's ESG performance. These innovations enable more accurate assessments and comparisons, making it easier to identify sustainable investment opportunities.

Machine learning and artificial intelligence (AI) are also being used to analyze large datasets, uncovering patterns and trends that human analysts might miss. These technologies can enhance the decision-making process and improve the accuracy of ESG ratings and forecasts.

Rise of Impact Investing

Impact investing goes beyond traditional ESG criteria by aiming to generate measurable social and environmental benefits alongside financial returns. Investors are increasingly looking to make a positive impact on issues such as poverty, education, healthcare, and environmental conservation.

Impact investing funds target companies and projects that address these challenges, providing capital to initiatives that deliver tangible, positive outcomes. This approach aligns financial goals with broader societal objectives, attracting a growing number of investors who seek both profit and purpose.

Integration of ESG in Passive Investing

The integration of ESG criteria into passive investing strategies is another notable trend. Historically, passive investing focused primarily on tracking market indices without considering ESG factors. However, the rise of ESG-focused index funds and ETFs allows investors to gain broad market exposure while adhering to sustainable principles.

These products track indices that include companies with strong ESG performance, offering a simple and cost-effective way for investors to incorporate sustainability into their portfolios. As demand for ESG-integrated passive investments grows, the range of available options continues to expand.

Regulatory Developments

Regulatory developments are playing a crucial role in shaping the landscape of sustainable investing. Governments and regulatory bodies worldwide are implementing policies and frameworks that promote transparency and accountability in ESG reporting. These regulations help standardize ESG disclosures, making it easier for investors to evaluate and compare companies.

For instance, the European Union's Sustainable Finance Disclosure Regulation (SFDR) requires financial market participants to disclose how they integrate ESG factors into their investment processes. Such regulations drive greater adoption of sustainable practices and enhance investor confidence in ESG data.

Innovation in Financial Products

Innovation in financial products is another driving force behind the growth of sustainable investing. New instruments and investment vehicles are being developed to meet the evolving needs of investors. Examples include sustainability-linked loans, where interest rates are tied to the borrower's ESG performance, and climate-themed funds that focus on companies combating climate change.

Additionally, digital platforms and fintech solutions are making sustainable investing more accessible to a broader audience. These platforms offer user-friendly interfaces, educational resources, and automated investment options that simplify the process of building a sustainable portfolio.

Corporate Commitment to ESG Goals

Companies are increasingly committing to ambitious ESG goals, recognizing that sustainable practices can enhance long-term profitability and resilience. Corporate initiatives such as setting science-based targets for carbon reduction, improving supply chain transparency, and fostering diversity and inclusion are becoming more common.

These commitments are often driven by stakeholder pressure, including demands from investors, customers, and employees. As a result, companies that prioritize ESG goals are better positioned to attract investment and build sustainable competitive advantages.

Collaboration and Partnerships

Collaboration and partnerships are essential for advancing sustainable investing. Asset managers, investors, NGOs, and other stakeholders are working together to develop best practices, share knowledge, and drive collective action. Initiatives like the United Nations Principles for Responsible Investment (UN PRI) provide a framework for integrating ESG considerations into investment decisions and encourage collaborative efforts to address global challenges.

Staying informed about these trends and innovations can help you navigate the evolving landscape of sustainable investing and make decisions that align with your financial goals and values. Embracing these developments allows you to contribute to positive social and environmental outcomes while pursuing long-term financial success.

Long-term Benefits

Investing with a focus on sustainability offers numerous long-term benefits that extend beyond immediate financial returns. These benefits can enhance the overall performance and resilience of your portfolio while contributing positively to society and the environment. Here are some key long-term advantages of sustainable investing.

Enhanced Financial Performance

Companies with strong environmental, social, and governance (ESG) practices often demonstrate better financial performance over the long term. These companies tend to be more efficient, have lower costs, and face fewer regulatory and legal risks. By prioritizing sustainability, they are better positioned to adapt to changing market conditions and consumer preferences, leading to more stable and robust financial returns.

Risk Mitigation

Sustainable investing helps mitigate various risks associated with traditional investments. Companies with poor ESG practices are more likely to encounter environmental fines, labor disputes, and governance scandals. By investing in companies with strong ESG credentials, you reduce the likelihood of being exposed to these risks. This leads to a more resilient portfolio that can better withstand economic and market fluctuations.

Alignment with Global Trends

Global trends are increasingly favoring sustainability. Governments, businesses, and consumers are becoming more environmentally conscious and socially responsible. Policies and regulations aimed at addressing climate change, promoting clean energy, and ensuring fair labor practices are becoming more prevalent. Investing in sustainable companies aligns your portfolio with these long-term trends, positioning you to benefit from future growth and opportunities in the green economy.

Positive Impact on Society and Environment

Sustainable investing allows you to contribute to positive societal and environmental change. By directing capital towards companies that prioritize sustainability, you support initiatives that address critical issues such as climate change, resource conservation, social equity, and ethical governance. This not only enhances your personal sense of fulfillment and purpose but also fosters a healthier, more equitable world for future generations.

Attracting Long-term Investors

Companies with strong ESG practices are increasingly attractive to long-term investors, including institutional investors, pension funds, and endowments. These investors seek stable, responsible companies that align with their values and offer reliable returns. As a result, sustainable companies often enjoy greater access to capital, improved investor relations, and a more stable shareholder base.

Encouraging Corporate Responsibility

Investing in sustainable companies encourages corporate responsibility and accountability. When investors prioritize ESG factors, they signal to companies that sustainability is essential. This can drive companies to adopt better practices, improve transparency, and enhance their overall performance. As more investors embrace sustainable investing, the collective impact can lead to widespread improvements in corporate behavior and industry standards.

Innovation and Competitive Advantage

Sustainable companies are often at the forefront of innovation. By focusing on sustainability, they develop new technologies, products, and services that meet the demands of an evolving market. This innovation can provide a competitive advantage, helping these companies capture market share, reduce costs, and drive long-term growth. As an investor, you benefit from being part of this dynamic and forward-thinking sector.

Long-term Value Creation

Sustainable investing is not just about avoiding risks; it's also about creating long-term value. Companies that integrate ESG factors into their strategies are better equipped to create sustainable value for their stakeholders. This holistic approach to business ensures that they consider the needs and expectations of their employees, customers, suppliers, and communities. Over time, this leads to stronger brand loyalty, enhanced reputation, and improved financial performance.

Building a Legacy

Sustainable investing allows you to build a legacy that reflects your values and aspirations. By prioritizing investments that promote positive change, you can make a lasting impact on the world. Whether you're investing for your own future, your family's future, or for charitable purposes, sustainable investing ensures that your capital is used to support a better, more sustainable world.

Investing with a focus on sustainability offers significant long-term benefits, including enhanced financial performance, risk mitigation, alignment with global trends, and positive societal impact. By embracing sustainable investing, you can build a resilient, future-oriented portfolio that not only delivers financial returns but also contributes to a more sustainable and equitable world.

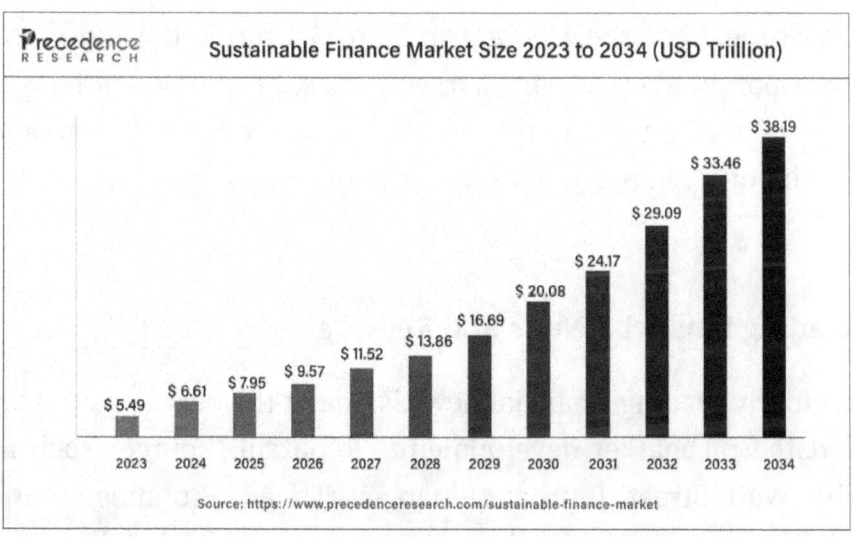

Sustainable Finance Market Size. Source: precedenceresearch.com

Chapter 10: Continuous Learning and Improvement

The Importance of Financial Education: Staying Informed

Staying informed is crucial for making sound investment decisions and keeping up with the ever-changing financial landscape. Access to accurate and timely information allows you to respond effectively to market trends, economic shifts, and new opportunities. Here's how you can stay informed and continuously improve your investment knowledge.

Reading Financial News and Reports

Regularly reading financial news is one of the best ways to stay updated on market developments. Reputable sources such as The Wall Street Journal, Financial Times, Bloomberg, and Reuters provide comprehensive coverage of global financial markets, economic data, and corporate news. Subscribing to these publications can give you daily insights into the factors influencing market movements.

Following Market Analysts and Experts

Many market analysts and financial experts share their insights through articles, blogs, and social media platforms. Following respected analysts can provide diverse perspectives on market conditions and investment strategies. Platforms like X (Twitter), LinkedIn, and specialized financial blogs are great places to find expert opinions and discussions.

Using Financial Websites and Tools

Websites like Yahoo Finance, Google Finance, and Investing.com offer a wealth of information, including real-time stock quotes, financial news, and analytical tools. These platforms allow you to track your portfolio, monitor market trends, and research individual stocks and sectors.

Watching Financial News Channels

Television channels like CNBC, Bloomberg TV, and Fox Business provide continuous coverage of financial markets. Watching these channels can help you stay informed about breaking news, market analysis, and interviews with industry leaders.

Subscribing to Newsletters

Many financial experts and investment firms offer newsletters that deliver market insights, analysis, and investment tips directly to your inbox. Subscribing to a few reputable newsletters can help you stay informed without having to actively search for information every day.

Attending Webinars and Seminars

Webinars and seminars conducted by financial experts and institutions offer valuable learning opportunities. These events often cover specific investment topics, market outlooks, and advanced strategies. Participating in these sessions can deepen your understanding and provide you with actionable insights.

Utilizing Investment Apps

Many investment apps provide news feeds, analysis, and alerts tailored to your portfolio. Apps like Robinhood, E*TRADE, and Fidelity offer features that help you stay informed about market changes and news affecting your investments.

Engaging in Online Communities

Online investment communities, such as forums and social media groups, can be a valuable resource for sharing ideas and gaining new perspectives. Websites like Reddit's r/investing or specialized investment groups on Facebook and LinkedIn allow you to interact with other investors, ask questions, and discuss market trends.

Reading Books and Research Papers

Investing in books written by experienced investors and financial experts can provide deeper insights into investment strategies and market theories. Research papers and academic journals also offer advanced knowledge on specific topics, helping you stay ahead of the curve.

Participating in Investment Courses

Enrolling in online investment courses can significantly enhance your knowledge and skills. Websites like Coursera, Udemy, and Khan Academy offer courses on various investment topics, from basic principles to advanced strategies. These courses often include interactive elements, quizzes, and practical exercises to reinforce learning.

Consulting Financial Advisors

Working with a financial advisor can provide personalized guidance tailored to your financial goals and risk tolerance.

Advisors have access to in-depth market research and can offer insights that are not always readily available to individual investors.

Staying informed is an ongoing process that requires dedication and curiosity. By leveraging multiple resources and continuously seeking new knowledge, you can make more informed investment decisions and adapt to changing market conditions effectively.

Continuous Learning

Continuous learning is essential for staying competitive and successful in the ever-evolving world of investing. The financial markets are dynamic, and keeping your knowledge up-to date helps you make informed decisions, adapt to new trends, and seize opportunities. Here are some effective strategies for maintaining a habit of continuous learning.

Engage with Educational Content

Investing in your education is crucial. Read books written by renowned investors and financial experts. Books like "The Intelligent Investor" by Benjamin Graham, "A Random Walk

Down Wall Street" by Burton Malkiel, and "One Up on Wall Street" by Peter Lynch offer timeless advice and insights into investment strategies and market behavior.

Take Online Courses

Online courses provide a structured way to deepen your knowledge. Platforms like Coursera, Udemy, and edX offer courses on a wide range of topics, from basic investing principles to advanced financial analysis. Enrolling in these courses can help you build a strong foundation and expand your expertise.

Attend Seminars and Workshops

Seminars and workshops offer opportunities to learn from experts and network with other investors. These events often cover specific investment topics, market outlooks, and advanced strategies. Participating in these sessions can provide practical insights and help you stay current with market developments.

Follow Market News and Analysis

Stay updated with the latest market news and analysis by regularly reading financial publications like The Wall Street Journal, Financial Times, and Bloomberg. These sources provide comprehensive coverage of global financial markets, economic data, and corporate news. Keeping up with market trends helps you understand the broader economic environment and its impact on your investments.

Use Financial Tools and Platforms

Leverage financial tools and platforms that offer educational resources. Websites like Yahoo Finance, Google Finance, and Investing.com provide access to financial news, stock quotes, and analysis tools. Many investment apps also offer educational content, tutorials, and market insights tailored to your portfolio.

Participate in Online Communities

Join online communities and forums where investors share ideas, discuss market trends, and provide mutual support. Websites like Reddit's r/investing, StockTwits, and specialized investment groups on Facebook and LinkedIn can be valuable resources for learning from others' experiences and gaining new perspectives.

Subscribe to Newsletters

Many financial experts and investment firms offer newsletters that deliver market insights, analysis, and investment tips directly to your inbox. Subscribing to reputable newsletters can help you stay informed about market trends and emerging opportunities without having to search for information actively.

Watch Financial News Channels

Television channels like CNBC, Bloomberg TV, and Fox Business provide continuous coverage of financial markets. Watching these channels can help you stay informed about breaking news, market analysis, and interviews with industry leaders, enhancing your understanding of current market conditions.

Engage with Financial Advisors

Consulting with a financial advisor can provide personalized guidance tailored to your financial goals and risk tolerance. Advisors have access to in-depth market research and can offer insights that may not be readily available to individual investors. Regular meetings with an advisor can help you stay on track and adjust your strategy as needed.

Reflect and Review

Regularly reflect on your investment decisions and review your portfolio's performance. Analyzing your successes and mistakes can provide valuable lessons and help you refine your investment strategy. Keeping a journal of your investment decisions and their outcomes can also aid in this reflective process.

Continuous learning is an ongoing commitment that requires dedication and curiosity. By engaging with diverse educational resources, staying updated with market developments, and seeking new knowledge, you can enhance your investment skills and achieve long-term financial success.

Resources for Investors: Books, Websites, and Courses

Continuous learning is essential for successful investing. There are numerous resources available to enhance your knowledge and skills, including books, websites, and courses. These tools can provide valuable insights, strategies, and up-to-date information to help you make informed investment decisions.

Books

Books are a foundational resource for deepening your understanding of investing. Many renowned investors and financial experts have written extensively on various aspects of investing, from basic principles to advanced strategies.

1. **"The Intelligent Investor" by Benjamin Graham:** This classic book is often considered the bible of value investing. It provides timeless wisdom on how to analyze stocks and build a solid investment strategy.

2. **"A Random Walk Down Wall Street" by Burton G. Malkiel:** This book introduces the efficient market hypothesis and the importance of diversification. It's a great resource for understanding modern investment theories.

3. **"Common Stocks and Uncommon Profits" by Philip Fisher:** Fisher's work focuses on qualitative analysis and finding companies with strong growth potential. It's a valuable read for growth investors.

4. **"One Up On Wall Street" by Peter Lynch:** Lynch shares his experiences and strategies for picking winning stocks, emphasizing the importance of doing your homework and investing in what you know.

Websites

There are numerous websites dedicated to providing financial news, data, and analysis. These platforms can help you stay updated on market trends, track your investments, and conduct research.

1. **Investopedia:** A comprehensive resource for learning about financial concepts, investment strategies, and market analysis. It offers articles, tutorials, and a financial dictionary to help you understand complex terms.

2. **Yahoo Finance:** Provides real-time stock quotes, financial news, and analysis. It's a useful tool for tracking your portfolio and staying informed about market movements.

3. **Morningstar:** Known for its in-depth analysis and ratings of mutual funds, stocks, and ETFs. Morningstar's research can help you evaluate investment opportunities and make informed decisions.

4. **Seeking Alpha:** Offers a platform for investors to share their analyses and opinions on various stocks and market trends. It's a great place to find diverse perspectives and investment ideas.

Courses

Online courses can provide structured learning and help you develop specific skills. Many platforms offer courses on investing, finance, and economics, catering to both beginners and advanced learners.

1. **Coursera:** Offers courses from top universities and institutions on a wide range of topics, including finance and investing. Courses like "Investment Management" by the University of Geneva provide comprehensive coverage of investment strategies and portfolio management.

2. **Udemy:** Features a variety of courses on investing, from stock market basics to advanced trading strategies. Courses are often taught by industry professionals and include practical exercises.

3. **Khan Academy:** Provides free educational content on economics and finance. Their finance and capital markets section covers the fundamentals of investing, making it accessible for beginners.

4. **edX:** Partners with universities to offer courses on investing and finance. For example, MIT's "Finance

Theory" course covers essential concepts in financial economics.

Utilizing These Resources

To make the most of these resources, consider setting aside dedicated time each week for learning. Start with foundational books to build your knowledge, then use websites to stay updated on current market conditions and deepen your understanding of specific topics. Enroll in online courses to gain structured knowledge and practical skills.

Balancing your learning across books, websites, and courses ensures you gain a comprehensive understanding of investing. This continuous learning approach will help you adapt to market changes, refine your strategies, and ultimately achieve your financial goals.

Networking and Professional Advice

Networking and seeking professional advice are essential components of a successful investment strategy. Building a network of knowledgeable individuals and consulting with financial experts can provide valuable insights, enhance your decision-making, and offer support in navigating complex financial markets.

Importance of Networking

Networking with other investors, industry professionals, and financial experts can significantly enhance your understanding of the markets. Engaging in discussions and sharing experiences with others helps you gain different perspectives and stay informed about new trends and opportunities.

Joining Investment Clubs

Investment clubs offer a structured environment for learning and collaboration. These clubs typically consist of a group of individuals who meet regularly to discuss investments, share research, and make collective decisions. Joining an investment club can provide you with a supportive community, access to diverse knowledge, and the opportunity to learn from more experienced investors.

Attending Industry Conferences

Industry conferences and seminars are excellent opportunities to network with professionals and learn about the latest developments in the financial world. These events often feature keynote speakers, panel discussions, and workshops led by industry leaders. Attending these conferences allows you to expand your network, gain new insights, and stay updated on market trends.

Leveraging Online Platforms

Online platforms and social media networks are valuable tools for networking and connecting with other investors. Platforms like LinkedIn, X (Twitter), and specialized investment forums offer opportunities to engage with experts, join discussions, and share ideas. Following industry influencers and participating in online communities can help you stay informed and build meaningful connections.

Consulting Financial Advisors

Professional financial advisors provide personalized guidance tailored to your financial goals and risk tolerance. They have access to extensive research, advanced tools, and market insights that can enhance your investment strategy. Regular consultations with an advisor can help you stay on track, adjust your portfolio as needed, and make informed decisions.

Choosing the Right Advisor

Selecting a financial advisor involves considering their qualifications, experience, and approach to investing. Look for advisors with relevant certifications, such as Certified Financial Planner (CFP) or Chartered Financial Analyst (CFA), and check their track record. It's also important to choose an advisor who aligns with your investment philosophy and communicates effectively.

Benefits of Professional Advice

Engaging with a financial advisor offers several benefits, including:

- **Objective Insights:** Advisors provide an unbiased perspective on your financial situation, helping you make rational decisions based on data and analysis.
- **Risk Management:** Advisors help you identify and manage risks, ensuring your portfolio remains balanced and aligned with your goals.

- **Access to Resources:** Advisors have access to exclusive research, investment products, and financial tools that can enhance your strategy.

- **Long-Term Planning:** Advisors assist with long-term financial planning, including retirement, estate planning, and tax strategies, ensuring you achieve your financial objectives.

Maintaining Professional Relationships

Building and maintaining relationships with financial professionals requires regular communication and engagement. Schedule periodic reviews with your advisor to discuss your portfolio's performance, market conditions, and any changes in your financial goals. Staying proactive in these relationships ensures you receive ongoing support and guidance.

Peer Learning and Collaboration

Collaborating with peers through study groups, online forums, or investment clubs facilitates shared learning and mutual support. Discussing strategies, analyzing market trends, and reviewing investment outcomes with peers can deepen your understanding and enhance your investment skills.

Networking and seeking professional advice are crucial for developing a well-rounded investment strategy. By building a network of knowledgeable individuals, participating in industry events, leveraging online platforms, and consulting with financial advisors, you can gain valuable insights, improve your decision-making, and achieve long-term financial success.

Reflecting on Your Investment Journey: Evaluating Your Progress

Regularly evaluating your progress is crucial to achieving your investment goals and ensuring your strategies remain effective. By systematically assessing your performance, you can identify strengths and weaknesses, make informed adjustments, and stay on track toward your financial objectives.

Setting Benchmarks

Start by setting clear benchmarks against which you can measure your progress. These benchmarks should be aligned with your financial goals and investment strategies. For instance, if your goal is to achieve a certain annual return, compare your portfolio's performance against that target and relevant market indices.

Reviewing Portfolio Performance

Evaluate your portfolio's performance regularly, at least quarterly. Examine the returns of individual investments and the overall portfolio. Consider both absolute performance (total returns) and relative performance (returns compared to benchmarks).

Pay attention to factors such as asset allocation, sector performance, and the impact of specific investment decisions. This analysis helps you understand which investments are contributing positively and which are underperforming.

Analyzing Risk and Volatility

Assess the risk and volatility of your portfolio. High returns are often accompanied by higher risk, so it's essential to ensure that your risk level aligns with your risk tolerance. Analyze metrics like standard deviation, beta, and Sharpe ratio to gauge the risk-adjusted performance of your investments.

Monitoring Progress Toward Goals

Track your progress toward your financial goals, such as retirement savings, purchasing a home, or funding education. Assess whether your current investment strategy is moving you closer to these goals. If you're falling short, consider whether you need to adjust your savings rate, investment choices, or time horizon.

Identifying Strengths and Weaknesses

Identify which aspects of your investment strategy are working well and which need improvement. For example, if your growth stocks are consistently outperforming but your fixed-income investments are lagging, you might need to re-evaluate your approach to bond selection.

Rebalancing Your Portfolio

Rebalancing involves adjusting your portfolio to maintain your desired asset allocation. Market fluctuations can cause your portfolio to drift from its original allocation, increasing risk. Regularly review and rebalance your portfolio to ensure it remains aligned with your investment objectives and risk tolerance.

Staying Informed

Continuous education is vital for staying informed about market trends, economic developments, and new investment opportunities. Regularly engage with financial news, research reports, and educational resources to keep your knowledge up to date. This ongoing learning process will help you make better investment decisions and adapt to changing market conditions.

Seeking Feedback and Professional Advice

Consider seeking feedback from trusted sources, such as financial advisors or investment mentors. They can provide an objective assessment of your strategy and suggest improvements. Professional advice can be particularly valuable for complex financial situations or when making significant changes to your investment approach.

Making Adjustments

Based on your evaluations, make necessary adjustments to your investment strategy. This might involve reallocating assets, diversifying into new sectors, or changing your investment horizon. Ensure that any changes are well-considered and aligned with your long-term goals.

Documenting Your Strategy

Keep a record of your investment strategy, including your goals, benchmarks, asset allocation, and any adjustments made. This documentation helps you stay disciplined and provides a reference for future evaluations. It also allows you to track your thought process and learn from past decisions.

Evaluating your progress regularly ensures that you stay on track toward your financial goals and make informed adjustments to your investment strategy. This proactive approach helps you navigate market changes, manage risks, and optimize your portfolio for long-term success.

Adjusting Your Strategies

Adapting your investment strategies in response to changing market conditions, personal circumstances, and financial goals is crucial for long-term success. Being flexible and responsive ensures that your portfolio remains aligned with your objectives and can navigate through various economic cycles.

Evaluating Market Conditions

Regularly assessing market conditions helps you understand the broader economic environment and its potential impact on your investments. Pay attention to key economic indicators such as GDP growth, inflation rates, and employment figures. Changes in these indicators can signal shifts in market trends and influence your investment strategy.

For example, in a rising interest rate environment, you might reduce exposure to long-term bonds, which are more sensitive to rate changes, and increase investments in sectors that benefit from higher rates, such as financials.

Reviewing Your Portfolio

Conduct periodic reviews of your portfolio to ensure it remains diversified and aligned with your risk tolerance and financial goals. This involves analyzing the performance of individual investments and the overall portfolio. Identify any underperforming assets and consider whether they should be held, sold, or replaced with better-performing investments.

Rebalancing your portfolio regularly helps maintain your desired asset allocation. This process involves selling overperforming assets and buying underperforming ones to restore balance, reducing risk and potentially enhancing returns.

Incorporating New Information

Stay informed about new developments and incorporate relevant information into your strategy. This includes changes in government policies, technological advancements, and shifts in consumer behavior. For instance, the growing emphasis on renewable energy might prompt you to increase investments in clean energy companies.

Adjusting to Personal Changes

Your personal circumstances and financial goals may change over time, necessitating adjustments to your investment strategy. Major life events such as marriage, having children, buying a home, or approaching retirement can impact your risk tolerance and investment horizon.

For example, as you near retirement, you might shift your portfolio towards more conservative investments like bonds and dividend-paying stocks to preserve capital and generate steady income.

Learning from Mistakes

Reflecting on past investment decisions, both successful and unsuccessful, provides valuable insights. Analyzing mistakes helps you understand what went wrong and how to avoid similar errors in the future. Keeping a journal of your investment decisions and their outcomes can aid in this reflective process.

Seeking Professional Guidance

Consulting with financial advisors can provide expert insights and tailored advice for adjusting your strategies. Advisors can help you navigate complex market conditions, optimize your portfolio, and ensure your investment strategy remains aligned with your long-term goals.

Implementing Risk Management Strategies

Effective risk management is essential for adapting your strategies. This includes setting stop-loss orders to limit potential losses, diversifying your portfolio to spread risk, and using hedging techniques to protect against market downturns. Maintaining a portion of your portfolio in cash or liquid assets can also provide a buffer during volatile periods and offer flexibility to take advantage of new opportunities.

Staying Flexible

Flexibility is key to adjusting your strategies successfully. Be open to exploring new investment opportunities and willing to make changes when necessary. This might involve experimenting with different asset classes, such as real estate, commodities, or cryptocurrencies, to enhance diversification and returns.

Monitoring Performance

Continuously monitor the performance of your investments and the overall portfolio. Use financial tools and platforms to track progress and make data-driven decisions. Regularly reviewing performance metrics helps you stay on top of your investments and make timely adjustments.

Adjusting your investment strategies is an ongoing process that requires vigilance, flexibility, and a proactive approach. By staying informed, regularly reviewing your portfolio, incorporating new information, and seeking professional guidance, you can adapt to changing conditions and achieve long-term financial success.

Conclusion

Investing is a journey that requires continuous learning, adaptability, and a strategic approach. Throughout this book, we have explored various aspects of investing, from understanding fundamental concepts to implementing advanced strategies. The goal has been to provide you with the knowledge and tools needed to navigate the complex world of finance and achieve your financial goals.

One of the key takeaways is the importance of setting clear financial goals. Whether you are saving for retirement, a new home, or your child's education, having specific objectives helps guide your investment decisions and keeps you focused on the long-term.

Diversification remains a cornerstone of effective investing. By spreading your investments across different asset classes, sectors, and geographic regions, you can reduce risk and enhance potential returns. It's not about avoiding risk entirely but managing it in a way that aligns with your risk tolerance and financial aspirations.

Staying informed is crucial. The financial markets are dynamic, influenced by a myriad of factors from economic indicators to geopolitical events. Regularly reading financial news, following expert analysis, and engaging in continuous learning will help you stay ahead and make informed decisions.

Adapting to change is another critical aspect. Markets will fluctuate, personal circumstances will evolve, and new opportunities will arise. Being flexible and willing to adjust your strategies ensures that your portfolio remains resilient and capable of weathering various economic cycles.

Networking and seeking professional advice can provide valuable insights and support. Engaging with other investors and consulting financial advisors can enhance your understanding and help you make more informed decisions.

Incorporating sustainable investing principles allows you to align your investments with your values, supporting companies that prioritize environmental, social, and governance factors. This not only contributes to positive societal impacts but can also enhance long-term financial performance.

Ultimately, successful investing is about balancing risk and reward, staying informed, and being proactive. By applying the principles and strategies discussed in this book, you can build a robust investment portfolio that supports your financial goals and adapts to an ever-changing world.

Thank you for taking this journey through the world of investing. May your financial future be bright and your investment decisions be wise.

Dear Reader,

I hope you found this book insightful and valuable.

Your feedback is invaluable to me. If you enjoyed this book, I would appreciate it if you could take a moment to leave a review on the reading apps and platforms.

Thank you for your support, and I wish you all the best.

Kind regards,
Ghazwan

About the Author

Ghazwan is a passionate entrepreneur and business strategist dedicated to helping individuals and organizations achieve their full potential with a deep understanding of modern businesses' challenges and opportunities.

With a Master's degree in Computer and Systems Sciences from Stockholm University, specializing in eService design, requirement engineering, and business process management, he is equipped to innovate cutting-edge solutions.

He believes in the power of collaboration and lifelong learning, and his mission is to empower people to reach their goals and positively impact the world.